# Everyday
# Vegetarian

EVERYDAY VEGETARIAN.

For information, address St. Martin's Press, 175 Fifth Avenue, New York, N.Y. 10010.

www.stmartins.com

Copyright © Elwin Street Limited 2015.

Conceived and produced by
Elwin Street Limited
3 Percy Street
London W1T 1DE
www.elwinstreet.com

Library of Congress Cataloging-in-Publication Data Available Upon Request

ISBN 978-1-250-06616-9 (trade paperback)
ISBN 978-1-250-06617-6 (e-book)

First U.S. Edition: June 2015

St. Martin's Griffin books may be purchased for educational, business, or promotional use. For information on bulk purchases, please contact Macmillan Corporate and Premium Sales Department at 1-800-221-7945, extension 5442, or write specialmarkets@macmillan.com.

10 9 8 7 6 5 4 3 2 1

Printed in Malaysia

# Everyday
## Vegetarian

365 days of healthy seasonal recipes

**Jane Hughes**

St. Martin's Griffin
New York

# Contents

# Foreword

*Len Torine, Executive Director of the
American Vegetarian Association (AVA)*

Vegetarianism has gone mainstream. No longer the bland bastion of an anti-carnivore subculture and fussy eaters, plant-based foods have become the darlings of the media, celebrity chefs, and the most savvy of our citizenry. Vegetarianism has become the proud symbol of a conscientious consumer.

These are not just committed vegetarians but also a group of aware "spillovers" who are interested in healthy living through meatless meals. The benefits of vegetarianism range from increased energy, more desirable cholesterol levels, lowered rates of obesity, an improved digestive tract, and more. The key is moderation and balance. Protein is readily available in beans, grains, and nuts; and vitamins, minerals, and fiber are abundant in most plant-based foods, such as leafy greens, tomatoes, citrus fruits, and root vegetables.

I sincerely believe *Everyday Vegetarian* will become the go-to book for enlightened foodies. Jane Hughes's passion and commitment to thorough research and ingredient ethics are clearly evident in each recipe. The book provides precisely what anyone considering any level of vegetarianism would need—a book you will use frequently, eventually earning its own proud patina of pages with plant-based food stains.

The true beauty and depth of *Everyday Vegetarian* is evidenced in its broad appeal. The easy-to-prepare recipes offer delightful dishes derived from a wide range of global cuisines, appropriate for health-minded chefs of any skill level. *Everyday Vegetarian* is definitely not just for the purists—carnivores and part-time vegetarians will absolutely enjoy these recipes as well.

# The Versatility of Vegetables

This collection of 365 recipes offers something fresh, healthy, and interesting for every single day of the year, making use of the fresh fruit, vegetables, and herbs that are in season and responding to natural patterns, with hearty dishes in winter, and light meals in the spring and summer. Recipes are grouped into seasonal sections, and within the sections they follow a sequence: soups, salads, and appetizers; main dishes; drinks and desserts. There are handy lists of the recipes at the beginning of each section, along with tips about which vegetables are available in each season of the year, and how to use them best.

As the seasons change, I hope you will enjoy browsing through each section of the book, reminding yourself of the ingredients that are at their freshest and most abundant, and savoring some classic flavor combinations—aromatic parsley and lemon with baby vegetables in spring; sweet, ripe tomatoes with gorgeous torn basil leaves in the summer; silky smooth squash soups with cinnamon and nutmeg in the fall; hearty bean stews with a spicy chili pepper kick in the wintertime. You'll find plenty of inspiration, whether you're looking for new variations on old favorites, or dishes you've never tried before. And of course, don't be afraid to mix and match—if you're in the mood for a lemon tart, whether it's spring, summer, fall, or winter, go for it, and enjoy the time you spend in the kitchen.

## Cook's Notes

Most of the following 365 recipes are suitable for beginners. Others provide a little more of a challenge, but none of the techniques are too difficult for an enthusiastic home cook. No special equipment is needed, but an inexpensive food processor will be invaluable for creating smooth soups, making breadcrumbs, chopping nuts, and blending chopped herbs into curry pastes, pestos, and sauces.

When cooking vegetarian and vegan foods, there are one or two things it's useful to know—for example, that many shop-bought desserts contain gelatin, which is an animal product, and that sometimes vegetable soups served in restaurants are made with meat-based bouillon. It's good to make your own so that you know exactly what you are eating! Some cheeses are also not suitable for vegetarians because they are made with animal rennet, so be sure to check the label.

Vegans don't consume any products that are derived from animals, including all dairy products, eggs, and honey. There are lots of vegan recipes in this book, but in many cases, it is also possible to "veganize" the vegetarian recipes by substituting vegan cheeses and non-dairy milks made with soy beans, almonds, or oats.

When creating a vegan recipe, remember that vegetable broths sometimes contain dairy products, pasta (especially fresh pasta) may contain eggs, and not all margarines are completely free from animal products—look for brands that are marked suitable for vegans.

 Look out for this symbol when planning vegan meals.

# Spring

## Soups, salads, and appetizers

## Mains and sides

## Drinks and sweets

# Fresh in Season ...

### Fava beans

Often the first fresh vegetable to be harvested in the spring, baby fava beans can be eaten in the pod. Later in the season, pod them and blanch them in boiling water, then rub off the greyish skins.

### Arugula

Quick and easy to grow, arugula is generally used as a salad leaf, but its distinctive peppery flavor also makes it a good choice for springtime soups and fresh pesto sauces to serve with pasta.

### Asparagus

Choose slender stems with tight buds. A traditional asparagus steamer allows you to stand the spears upright in just a little water. This technique makes the stems tender without getting the delicate tips soggy.

### Artichokes

Look for firm, medium-sized heads and leaves that are crisp. You will be discarding all but the heart and the most tender inner leaves, but the outer appearance gives good clues about the size and freshness of the center.

### Peas

Sweet and tender peas can be eaten raw, straight from the pod, or cooked for just a couple of minutes in boiling salted water. Unblemished pods can be used to make pea pod soup or even a traditional country wine.

### Broccoli

Choose large, dense heads with no sign of yellowing, and use them soon after buying, as they don't keep well. The stems are edible—peel them with a potato peeler, cut into matchsticks or slices and add to a stir-fry.

### Watercress

The peppery flavor of watercress makes it a welcome addition to the seasonal salad bowl. Try it in chilled soups, or use it in place of spinach to make pâtés or spanakopita, a Greek-style dish with salty feta cheese encased in crisp phyllo pastry.

### Baby vegetables

The earliest little carrots, zucchini and leeks look very pretty served whole as crudités. Steam them gently to serve hot on top of a bowl of pasta or rice. The season's freshest herbs are ideal partners for baby vegetables.

# 1 Chili pepper and cilantro cakes

Makes 8

## Ingredients

- 1 pound potatoes
- 1 large egg
- 6 scallions
- 1 red chili pepper
- 2 ounces Cheddar cheese
- Handful fresh cilantro
- Zest 1 lime
- ⅔ cup Japanese panko bread crumbs
- 2 tablespoons canola oil, for drizzling

## Preparation

Peel the potatoes and boil them in salted water until soft. Drain and set aside to dry out a little. Separate the egg into white and yolk. Trim and finely chop the scallions. De-seed and finely chop the chili pepper. Shred the cheese. Chop the cilantro.

Mash the potatoes with the egg yolk, scallions, lime zest, chopped chili pepper, Cheddar cheese, and cilantro.

Preheat the oven to 400°F. Beat the egg white a little and put it into a saucer. Put the bread crumbs onto a plate.

Shape the mashed potato into small flattened cakes, and dip first in the egg white and then in the bread crumbs. Place on a lightly greased baking sheet and drizzle with the canola oil. Bake for 20 minutes until crisp and golden.

# 2 Garlic, pea, and fava bean dip

Serves 4

## Ingredients

- 2 cups fresh peas
- 2 cups fresh fava beans
- ¼ cup olive oil
- 2 cloves garlic
- 1 lemon
- Salt and freshly ground black pepper

## Preparation

Bring a large pan of salted water to a boil, add the peas and beans and cook for three minutes. Drain and refresh under cold water. Warm the olive oil in a skillet. Peel and chop the garlic and sauté it very gently for three minutes. Zest the lemon and squeeze out the juice.

Put the peas and beans into a food processor with the garlic and the olive oil, the lemon zest, and lemon juice. Blend to a purée and season well to taste. Serve as a dip, or spread onto toasted ciabatta slices.

## 3 Roasted red bell pepper and tomato soup

Serves 4

### Ingredients

- 2 red bell peppers
- 1 onion
- 1 pound tomatoes
- 3 tablespoons olive oil
- 1 tablespoon balsamic vinegar
- 1 ¼ cups 2% milk
- ½ teaspoon brown sugar

### Preparation

Preheat the oven to 375°F. Cut the bell peppers into quarters and discard the seeds and white pith. Peel the onion and chop into quarters. Cut the tomatoes in half. Put the vegetables in a large mixing bowl and stir in the olive oil and vinegar, making sure that all the pieces are well covered. Transfer the vegetables to a baking tray and roast for 30 minutes, until beginning to brown.

Allow the vegetables to cool, then blend in a blender, adding sufficient water to make a thick purée. Transfer the mixture to a sauce pan and stir in the milk and the sugar. Warm through and add more water if necessary to achieve your ideal consistency.

*Many roasted vegetables can be made into soup this way. If you are using the oven for a different recipe, consider roasting some vegetables at the same time. Store the vegetables in the refrigerator, and you can make a delicious soup in minutes!*

## 4 Edamame fritters with wasabi

Serves 4

### Ingredients

- 2 large eggs
- 1 teaspoon wasabi powder
- 2 cloves garlic
- 1 inch ginger root
- 1 cup all-purpose flour
- Sea salt
- 3 cups fresh or frozen edamame beans
- Vegetable oil, for the pan

### Preparation

Beat the eggs. Mix the wasabi powder with a little water to make a paste. Peel and crush the garlic. Shred the ginger, then gather up the pieces and squeeze them over a small bowl to collect the juice. Discard the pulp.

Put the flour and a pinch of salt into a large bowl, and beat in the eggs, wasabi paste, garlic, and ginger juice. Mix the edamame beans thoroughly into the batter.

Pour the oil into a deep skillet, to a depth of around ½ inch. Heat the oil until a little batter dropped into it sizzles straight away. Gently fry small spoonfuls of the edamame mixture, until crisp and golden on both sides.

*Edamame are fresh green soy beans, popped out of their pods. Rich in protein, they also make a great addition to salads.*

## 5 Crudités with sherry vinaigrette

Serves 4

### Ingredients
- 1 ½ ounces mixed fresh, colorful baby vegetables: carrots, radishes, asparagus spears, baby fennel

### For the dressing
- 1 shallot
- ⅓ cup extra-virgin olive oil
- 2 tablespoons sherry vinegar
- 1 teaspoon Dijon mustard
- ½ teaspoon coarse-ground salt

### Preparation
Make the dressing first. Peel the shallot and chop it as finely as you can. Mix it with the oil and vinegar, mustard and salt.

Trim and rinse the vegetables—it should not be necessary to peel them. Cut any that are large into bite-size pieces.

In a large bowl, mix the vegetables with the dressing, cover and chill for at least three hours—overnight is fine. Toss again before serving.

*This classic French vinaigrette brings out the flavor of each vegetable without the need for any further dips.*

## 6 Tomato and basil bruschetta

Serves 4

### Ingredients
- 1 small French baguette or similar style Italian bread
- 1 ½ ripe tomatoes
- ⅔ cup black pitted olives
- 2 cloves garlic
- Few sprigs fresh basil
- 1 tablespoon olive oil, plus extra to serve
- 1 teaspoon balsamic vinegar
- Few fresh chives
- Salt and freshly ground black pepper

### Preparation
Slice the bread and toast it lightly on both sides. Roughly chop the tomatoes, slice the olives and peel and crush the garlic. Strip the basil leaves from their stalks and tear roughly.

Mix the tomatoes, olives, and garlic together in a large bowl with the basil, olive oil and balsamic vinegar. Top each slice of bread with a generous spoonful of the tomato mixture. Trim and chop the chives into 1-inch pieces, or leave whole, to garnish.

Finish the dish with freshly ground salt and black pepper, and an extra drizzle of olive oil.

# 7 Miso and soba soup

Serves 4

### Ingredients

- 3 ounces dried soba noodles
- 2 ounces firm tofu
- 3 scallions
- Handful fresh cilantro
- 3 tablespoons miso paste
- Pinch dried red pepper flakes

### Preparation

Bring a 3-quart pan of salted water to a boil and cook the noodles for up to eight minutes, until tender. Drain and refresh under cold running water.

Drain and press the tofu, and cut into small cubes. Trim and chop the scallions. Finely chop the cilantro.

In a separate, 3-quart pan, bring 4¼ cups of water to a boil. Remove from the heat. Put the miso into a small bowl or cup and stir in a little of the hot water to make a runny paste. Stir this back into the pan of hot water, tasting after each addition, until the strength suits your taste. Stir in the tofu.

Divide the cooked noodles between two to four serving bowls, cover with the soup and top with the chopped onions, cilantro and red pepper flakes.

*In Japanese, the word soba is synonymous with both the grain buckwheat and these buckwheat noodles. The noodles are thin (unlike the thicker udon noodles) and are often served in soups or chilled with a dipping sauce. By not boiling this nutritious soup after adding the miso, you will preserve more of the valuable B vitamins that it contains.*

# 8 Quick minestrone

Serves 4

### Ingredients

- 1 onion
- 2 carrots
- 2 potatoes
- 2 leeks
- 2 ribs celery
- ½ pound green beans
- 1 pound tomatoes
- 2 zucchini
- 4 ounces pasta: penne or fusilli
- Large sprig fresh rosemary
- 1 x 15-ounce can of red kidney beans
- Salt and freshly ground black pepper

### Preparation

Peel the onion, carrots, and potatoes, and trim the leeks and celery ribs. Finely chop them all and put in a 4-quart pan with 5 pints boiling water. Simmer for 10 minutes.

Trim and chop the green beans, and chop the tomatoes. Trim and dice the zucchini. Add these vegetables to the pot along with the pasta, rosemary, and drained, rinsed kidney beans. Season with salt and pepper and cook until the pasta is cooked through.

## 9 Essential lemon oil

Serves 4

### Ingredients

- 2 unwaxed lemons
- 1 cup olive oil

### Preparation

Zest the lemons. Place the zest with the oil in a small pan and warm gently for three minutes. Remove from the heat and let cool. Transfer to a bowl, cover, and infuse for 24 hours. Strain the oil into a sterilized bottle and store in the refrigerator for up to a month.

*Olive oil begins to solidify when it is stored in the refrigerator, so you will need to allow it to come to room temperature before using. Try drizzling it over some freshly steamed asparagus spears.*

## 10 Herbal vinegar

Serves 4

### Ingredients

- Fresh herbs of your choice: basil, lemon balm, rosemary, mint, oregano, and bay leaves are all good
- Sufficient white wine vinegar or cider vinegar to fill your chosen bottle(s)

### Preparation

Wash and dry the fresh herbs gently to avoid bruising them, and pack them into a sterilized jar. Fill the jar with vinegar, seal, and store in a dark place at room temperature. Leave for between three and six weeks, depending on how strong you want the taste to be.

Strain the vinegar through a cheesecloth and transfer to a freshly sterilized bottle. Add one or two fresh sprigs of one of your chosen herbs before sealing.

# 11 Red pepper caponata with green olives

Serves 4

### Ingredients

- 8 red bell peppers
- ²⁄₃ cup extra-virgin olive oil
- 1 cup cocktail onions
- 1 ¼ cups green olives
- Salt and freshly ground black pepper
- Handful fresh parsley

### Preparation

De-seed the bell peppers and thinly slice. Warm the olive oil in a pan, add the peppers and mix well so that they are covered in oil. Cover the pan and turn the heat to the lowest possible setting. Cook for 20 minutes, stirring occasionally.

Slice away and discard the bases of the onions. Put the onions into a large bowl of boiling water. Leave for three minutes, before scooping out with a slotted spoon. The onions should separate easily into individual "leaves."

Arrange the warm bell peppers and oil on a serving dish, with the onion pieces and green olives on top. Season generously with salt and pepper. Chop the fresh parsley and sprinkle over the warm caponata before serving.

*Caponata originated as a Sicilian salad made from cooked eggplant and capers, but the term has since come to be used for all sorts of salads, served warm or chilled, that are made with soft-cooked Mediterranean-style vegetables.*

## 12 Warm arugula, mushroom, and snap pea salad

Serves 4

### Ingredients
- ½ pound sugar snap peas
- ½ pound red bell pepper
- ½ pound arugula
- 1 pound mushrooms
- ¼ stick salted butter

### For the dressing
- 1 inch ginger root
- Sprig fresh thyme
- 3 tablespoons cider vinegar
- ⅓ cup olive oil
- 1 clove garlic

### Preparation
Start by making the dressing. Shred the ginger and then squeeze out the juice. Discard the pulp. Strip the thyme leaves from their stalks and chop. Put the olive oil, cider vinegar, ginger juice, thyme, and garlic in a blender or food processor and process until smooth.

Steam the sugar snap peas for three minutes—they should be bright green and still quite crisp. Refresh them under cold running water. De-seed and roughly chop the red bell pepper. Put in a large mixing bowl with the sugar snap peas. Roughly chop the arugula and add to the bowl.

Wipe and slice the mushrooms. Melt the butter in a skillet and sauté the mushrooms gently for about eight minutes. Stir the warm mushrooms into the salad. Toss the dressing through the vegetables and serve immediately.

*This salad is best eaten when the mushrooms are still warm. The butter they are cooked in can go into the salad, too.*

## 13 Rhubarb, pecan, and goat cheese salad

Serves 4

### Ingredients
- 3 ribs rhubarb
- 2 tablespoons sugar
- ⅓ cup pecans
- 6 ounces mixed salad
- 2 ounces goat cheese

### For the dressing
- 1 shallot
- 2 tablespoons balsamic vinegar
- 1 tablespoon canola oil
- Salt and freshly ground black pepper

### Preparation
Preheat the oven to 450°F.

Trim the rhubarb and cut into ½-inch chunks. Put in a mixing bowl and toss with the sugar. Transfer to a baking sheet lined with parchment paper and bake for five minutes, until just starting to soften.

Roughly chop the pecans. Toast them in a dry, heavy skillet for a few minutes, until aromatic and beginning to brown.

To make the dressing, peel the shallot and chop it very finely. Beat with the remaining dressing ingredients.

Toss the dressing through the salad and arrange on a large serving plate topped with the rhubarb, crumbled cheese, and nuts.

## 14 Avocado and farfalle salad with mint

Serves 4

### Ingredients
- ½ pound pasta: farfalle or fusilli work well
- 2 ripe avocados
- 1 lime
- Handful fresh mint
- 1 red chili pepper
- 2 tablespoons olive oil
- Salt and freshly ground black pepper

### Preparation
Bring a 4-quart pan of salted water to a boil and cook the pasta until just tender. Refresh under cold running water and set to one side.

Peel and pit the avocados. Zest and juice the lime. Finely chop the mint. De-seed and finely chop the chili pepper. Reserve half an avocado, and mash the rest together with the lime juice and zest, mint, chili pepper, olive oil, and seasoning. Dice or slice the reserved avocado half.

Toss the avocado mixture through the pasta and serve immediately, topped with the reserved avocado pieces.

## 15 Chickpea and grape salad with citrus dressing

Serves 4

### Ingredients

- 2 cups sprouted chickpeas
- 2 cups seedless grapes
- Handful fresh parsley
- ½ teaspoon fennel seeds
- ⅓ cup sunflower seeds

### For the dressing

- 1 orange
- 1 lemon
- 2 teaspoons Dijon mustard
- 2 tablespoons flaxseed oil
- 2 teaspoons cider vinegar
- Freshly ground black pepper

### Preparation

Make the dressing first. Cut the orange and lemon in half and remove the seeds. Chop them into smaller pieces, keeping the skins on. Purée in a blender with the remaining dressing ingredients, adding a little extra water or orange juice if necessary, to make a pourable dressing.

Rinse the sprouted chickpeas and cut the grapes in half. Finely chop the parsley. Transfer the salad ingredients to a large bowl and toss the dressing through immediately before serving.

## 16 Blue cheese and walnut salad

Serves 4

### Ingredients

- ½ pound mixed salad
- ¾ cup walnut pieces
- 4 ounces vegetarian blue cheese
- 3 tablespoons walnut oil
- 2 tablespoons cider vinegar

### Preparation

Divide the salad between four serving plates and top with the walnuts and crumbled cheese. Beat the oil and vinegar together and serve separately so that guests can dress their own salad.

*Not all blue cheeses are suitable for vegetarians—Gorgonzola, for example, is made with animal rennet. Be sure to read the label before you buy.*

# 17 Superfood salad

Serves 4

### Ingredients

- 2 tablespoons quinoa
- ½ pound broccoli
- 4 ounces cucumber
- 1 lemon
- Handful fresh, flat-leaf parsley
- Handful fresh mint
- 1 avocado
- ½ cup alfalfa sprouts
- 3 tablespoons olive oil
- 4 ounces feta cheese
- 1 tablespoon pumpkin seeds
- Pinch sumac
- Salt and freshly ground black pepper

### Preparation

Bring a pan of salted water to a boil. Cook the quinoa for up to 15 minutes, until tender. Drain and spread on a plate to cool.

Chop the broccoli into bite-size pieces. Chop the cucumber into batons. Zest and juice the lemon. Roughly chop the herbs. Just before you are ready to serve the salad, peel and chop the avocado—it will begin to brown if you prepare it too early.

Transfer the quinoa into a large mixing bowl and stir in the broccoli, cucumber, avocado, alfalfa sprouts, and chopped herbs. Add the lemon zest and juice and the olive oil, and toss together. Top each portion of the salad with crumbled feta cheese, pumpkin seeds, a dusting of sumac, and salt and pepper.

# 18 Ginger and sesame wakame salad

Serves 4

### Ingredients

- 1 ounce dried wakame
- 1 clove garlic
- ½ inch ginger root
- ½ red chili pepper
- 2 tablespoons soy sauce
- 2 tablespoons honey
- 1 tablespoon lemon juice
- 1 teaspoon toasted sesame oil

### Preparation

Soak the wakame in cold water for an hour, then drain and finely shred. Peel and crush the garlic. Peel and finely chop the ginger. De-seed the red chili pepper and finely chop.

Mix all the ingredients thoroughly and chill for an hour before serving.

*Wakame is a Japanese seaweed with a subtle, sweet taste. It is sold dried, and can be crumbled over foods or rehydrated and added to salads*

## 19 Spicy marinated daikon salad

Serves 4

### Ingredients

- 14 ounces daikon
  (Japanese white radish)
- 1 red bell pepper
- 2 scallions
- 1 date

### For the dressing

- ½ red chili pepper
- 1 clove garlic
- ½ inch ginger root
- 1 tablespoon soy sauce
- 2 tablespoons cider vinegar
- 2 teaspoons honey
- 1 tablespoon toasted sesame oil

### Preparation

Peel the daikon and chop it into matchsticks. Finely dice the red bell pepper, and trim and chop the scallions. Finely chop the date. Place these ingredients in a large bowl.

To make the dressing, de-seed the red chili pepper and chop it very finely. Peel and crush the garlic. Peel the ginger and chop it very finely. Combine with the remaining dressing ingredients, adding a little cold water to achieve the desired consistency.

Toss the dressing through the salad and chill for an hour before serving.

*Top each portion with a little finely shredded red cabbage or carrot to add a splash of color to this refreshing salad.*

## 20 Blueberry, blue cheese, and watercress salad

Serves 4

### Ingredients

- 3 ounces watercress
- 3 ounces baby spinach
- ¾ cup blueberries
- 3 ounces vegetarian blue cheese

### For the dressing

- ¾ cup blueberries
- 1 tablespoon balsamic vinegar
- 1 tablespoon honey
- 3 tablespoons olive oil

### Preparation

Make the dressing first. Put all the ingredients in a blender or food processor and blend until smooth.

Wash and roughly chop the watercress and spinach. Put in a large bowl. Toss the blueberries and the dressing through the salad. Transfer the salad to a large serving plate, top with crumbled blue cheese and serve immediately.

# 21 Vegetable tempura with citrus dipping sauce

Serves 4

### Ingredients
- 2 red bell peppers
- 1 green bell pepper
- 2 small onions
- 6 scallions
- Vegetable oil for deep frying

### For the batter
- 1 cup all-purpose flour
- 1 tablespoon cornstarch
- ½ cup sparkling mineral water
- Pinch salt

### For the dipping sauce
- 3 tablespoons soy sauce
- 3 tablespoons mirin (Japanese rice wine)
- Juice 1 orange
- 1 teaspoon sugar

### Preparation

Beat all the batter ingredients together to make a smooth, thin batter. Make the dipping sauce by mixing all the ingredients together in a small bowl and stirring until the sugar is dissolved.

De-seed the peppers and cut into bite-size pieces. Peel and slice the onions into rings. Trim the scallions.

Heat the oil in a 4-quart pan or large wok. Dip the prepared vegetables into the batter and sauté in small batches—don't overload the pan as this will lower the temperature of the oil and make your tempura soggy. Drain on paper towels and serve immediately with the dipping sauce.

*This dish is best served as an appetizer, snack or side dish rather than the centerpiece of a meal. You can also use vegetables such as zucchini, carrots, or broccoli here—just chop into small pieces first.*

## 22 Fattoush salad

Serves 4

### Ingredients

- 1 pound whole small fava beans
- 1 cucumber
- Small bunches of fresh mint, parsley, and chives
- 2 whole-wheat pita breads
- 1 lemon
- ¼ cup olive oil
- 1 teaspoon honey (plus extra to garnish)
- 4 ounces feta cheese
- Freshly ground black pepper

### Preparation

Bring a large pan of salted water to a boil and cook the beans for three minutes. Drain and refresh under cold water, then pop the bright green beans out of their gray-green skins and discard the skins.

Trim and chop the cucumber, and finely chop the herbs. Toast the pita breads and then tear them into bite-size pieces. Zest and juice the lemon, and whisk together with the olive oil and honey.

Transfer all the ingredients to a large mixing bowl, toss together gently and top with crumbled feta cheese, freshly ground black pepper and a final drizzle of honey.

*Fattoush is a traditional bread salad from the Middle East. Fava beans provide another texture and a little extra goodness!*

## 23 Layered beet salad

Serves 4

### Ingredients

- 3 beets
- 3 carrots
- 1 small red cabbage
- ½ red onion
- 2 tablespoons olive oil
- 2 tablespoons balsamic vinegar

### Preparation

Peel the beets and carrots, and trim the outer leaves and core of the cabbage. Shred them all separately. Peel the onion and slice it as thinly as you can. Mix the oil and vinegar together to make the salad dressing.

To serve, layer the shredded carrot, beets and cabbage into small glass bowls, or pile onto a large serving plate. You can mix them together, but it looks nicer if you keep each ingredient separate, and you can taste their individual flavors too. Garnish with the finely sliced red onions and the balsamic dressing.

*If you can find golden beets or purple carrots, this is the perfect way to showcase their unusual colors.*

# 24 Pea pakoras

Serves 4

### Ingredients
- 1 pound potatoes
- ½ pound fresh or frozen peas
- 1 teaspoon ground coriander
- 1 teaspoon ground cumin
- ½ teaspoon chili powder

### Preparation
Preheat the oven to 400°F.

Peel the potatoes and cut them into small chunks. Heat a large pan of salted water and boil the potatoes for up to 15 minutes, until cooked through. Add the peas to cook in the same pan for the last five minutes. Use a slotted spoon to retrieve around half of the peas, and set these aside. Drain the remaining peas with the potatoes and mash them together with the ground coriander, cumin, and chili powder. Stir in the reserved whole peas.

Form the mixture into 16 to 20 small balls and put on a baking sheet lined with parchment paper. Bake for 20 minutes, until crisp and golden.

*Pakoras are fried savory snacks, most commonly a mixture of vegetables dipped in a batter made with chickpea flour. Pakoras are thought to have originated in India but are popular across southern Asia.*

## 25 Onion and potato bhajis

Makes 8

### Ingredients

- 3 onions
- 1 potato
- Few sprigs fresh cilantro
- 1 teaspoon garam masala
- 1 cup chickpea (gram) flour
- Canola oil, for the pan

### Preparation

Peel the onions and finely chop. Peel the potato and coarsely shred it. Chop the cilantro. Mix the onion, potato, cilantro, garam masala, and chickpea flour together thoroughly to form a stiff dough.

Heat the oil in a skillet and fry flattened teaspoons of the mixture gently on both sides for about eight minutes, until cooked through and crisp.

*Bhajis are a popular street food in India. They are deep-fried snacks made from shredded onion (or other vegetables) mixed with a batter made from chickpea flour.*

# 26 Cashew nut croquettes

Makes 12

## Ingredients

- 1 large egg
- 1 ¾ pounds potatoes
- 1 tablespoon salted butter
- Salt and freshly ground black pepper
- 1 cup cashew nuts
- 2 tablespoons all-purpose flour
- 2 tablespoons canola oil

## Preparation

Separate the egg into yolk and white.

Peel the potatoes, boil them in salted water for up to 20 minutes, until soft. Drain and mash them with the butter, seasoning, and egg yolk. Let cool.

Put the cashews into a dry, heavy pan and heat them gently, stirring frequently, until they begin to color. Turn them onto a chopping board and, when cool enough, finely chop.

Beat the egg white lightly and put it into a saucer. Put the chopped nuts onto a plate.

Preheat the oven to 400°F. Working on a floured surface, roll the mashed potato into croquette shapes, ensure that they are coated with flour, and then dip them into the egg white. Next, dip them into the chopped nuts and make sure the surfaces are covered. Put on a lightly greased baking sheet.

When all the croquettes have been made, drizzle them with canola oil and bake for 20 minutes, until golden.

# 27 Braised lettuce with creamy scallion dip

Serves 4

## Ingredients

- 2 baby romaine lettuces
- 1 bunch scallions
- ¼ stick salted butter
- 2 tablespoons olive oil
- 2 teaspoons all-purpose flour
- 1 cup plus 2 tablespoons vegetable bouillon
- 1¾ cups fresh peas
- Salt and freshly ground black pepper
- Juice 1 lemon

### For the dip

- 1 bunch scallions
- 1¾ cups sour cream
- Salt and freshly ground black pepper

### Preparation

Trim the lettuce stalks and slice the lettuce from base to tip, about ½-inch thick. Trim and finely chop the scallions.

Melt the butter with the oil in a 3-quart heavy pan. Stir in the flour, cook for a few seconds and then gradually add the vegetable bouillon, stirring constantly to prevent any lumps from forming.

Add the lettuce, peas, and scallions, season with a little salt and pepper and simmer, covered, for 10 minutes, until the vegetables are tender. Add the lemon juice just before serving.

To make the dip, trim the scallions and chop very finely. Stir into the sour cream and season to taste with salt and pepper.

*This simple dip is also perfect with fresh crudités.*

## 28 Golden baby potatoes
Serves 4

### Ingredients
- 1 pound baby potatoes
- 3 onions
- Few sprigs fresh thyme
- Small handful fresh parsley
- ¼ stick salted butter
- 2 bay leaves
- 2 tablespoons olive oil
- Salt and freshly ground black pepper

### Preparation
Boil the baby potatoes in salted water for about 25 minutes, until tender. Drain and set aside. Peel and finely slice the onions. Strip the thyme leaves from the stalks. Chop the parsley.

Melt the butter in a 3-quart heavy pan and stir in the onions, thyme leaves, and bay leaves. Cover, turn the heat to minimum and cook for up to 20 minutes, until the onions are very soft. Then turn up the heat and stir for a few more minutes, until golden.

Slice or halve the baby potatoes and stir them into the onions along with the olive oil. Fry until golden, around 10 minutes. Stir the chopped parsley into the dish immediately before serving and season with salt and freshly ground black pepper.

## 29 Spring vegetables with red pesto
Serves 4

### Ingredients
- ½ pound baby potatoes
- ½ pound baby carrots
- 6 ounces baby zucchini
- 8 shallots
- 3 ounces baby asparagus spears
- 3 ounces fine green beans

### For the pesto
- 2 tomatoes
- Handful fresh basil
- 2 cloves garlic
- 2 ounces vegetarian Parmesan-style cheese
- 1 tablespoon olive oil

### Preparation
Bring a pan of salted water to a boil and cook the potatoes for up to 15 minutes, until tender. Trim the remaining vegetables and chop into bite-size pieces, then steam them for 10 minutes, until just tender.

To make the pesto, roughly chop the tomatoes and basil. Peel and crush the garlic, and shred the cheese. Put all the ingredients into a food processor, and process to a rough paste.

Toss the cooked vegetables with the pesto and serve immediately.

## 30 Curried baby potatoes

Serves 4

### Ingredients

- 12 ounces baby potatoes
- 1 onion
- 1 inch ginger root
- 2 tablespoons vegetable oil
- ½ teaspoon turmeric
- ½ teaspoon cumin seeds
- ½ teaspoon cayenne pepper
- Juice ½ lemon
- Pinch salt
- 1 tablespoon fresh, chopped cilantro

### Preparation

Parboil the potatoes until they are not quite softened. Drain and cut into bite-size pieces.

Peel and roughly chop the onion. Peel and shred the ginger. Warm the oil in a large skillet and gently sauté the onion and ginger for five minutes, until the onion is soft and translucent. Stir in the turmeric, cumin seeds, and cayenne. Mix well, add the potatoes and cook, stirring constantly, for five more minutes. Stir in the lemon juice, salt, and chopped fresh cilantro and serve hot, as a side dish or wrapped in Crispy Chickpea Crêpes (see page 47).

## 31 Stir-fried baby vegetables with water chestnuts

Serves 4

### Ingredients

- 2 pounds mixed fresh baby vegetables: carrots, scallions, summer squash
- 1 onion
- 1 cup water chestnuts
- 4 cloves garlic
- 1½ inch ginger root
- 3 tablespoons toasted sesame oil
- 3 tablespoons soy sauce

### Preparation

Trim and rinse the vegetables, and finely slice. Peel and slice the onion. Slice the water chestnuts. Peel the garlic and slice each clove from top to bottom to make as many thin slices as you can. Peel and shred the ginger.

Put the soy sauce and sesame oil into a large pan or wok and stir-fry all the ingredients together on high heat, stirring constantly, for up to five minutes, until the vegetables are heated through but still crisp. Serve immediately.

# 32 Spring vegetables with orange and fennel seeds

Serves 4

### Ingredients

- 4 pounds fresh mixed baby vegetables: carrots, fennel, bok choy, asparagus
- 1 orange
- 2 teaspoons fennel seeds
- ¼ cup extra-virgin olive oil
- Few sprigs fresh parsley

### Preparation

Trim and rinse the vegetables—it should not be necessary to peel them, and the carrots are attractive with some of their greenery left intact. Cut any large vegetables into crudité-size sticks. Juice and zest the orange. Crush the fennel seeds with a pestle and mortar or a rolling pin, mix together with the olive oil, orange juice, and orange zest, and combine all the ingredients in a large bowl. Chill for 20 minutes. Chop the fresh parsley and stir into the vegetables before serving.

*Fennel seeds have a delicate aniseed flavor and are said to aid digestion and settle the stomach. To ensure the fennel seeds do not scatter when crushed with a rolling pin, cover them with plastic wrap.*

## 33 Gingered collard greens

Serves 4

### Ingredients

- 1 pound collard greens: chard, mustard greens, dandelion greens, and kale are all good
- 1 inch ginger root
- 1 clove garlic
- 1 tablespoon olive oil
- 1 tablespoon cider vinegar
- 1 tablespoon soy sauce
- 2 tablespoons toasted sesame oil
- 1 tablespoon sesame seeds

### Preparation

Wash the greens and discard any woody stems or discolored leaves. Finely shred the greens. Peel and finely chop the ginger. Peel and crush the garlic.

In a 3-quart pan or wok, warm the olive oil and sauté the ginger and garlic over a gentle heat for one minute, then stir in the vinegar and soy sauce. Raise the heat to medium and add the greens and 2 tablespoons of water. Cover and cook for five minutes, then remove the lid, toss the greens to ensure that they cook evenly and cook, uncovered, for a further three minutes until tender. Remove the pan or wok from the heat, and drain off any excess cooking liquid before serving.

Drizzle each portion with sesame oil and top with a sprinkling of sesame seeds.

## 34 Quinoa with currants and spicy onions

Serves 4

### Ingredients

- 2 cups quinoa
- ½ cup zante currants or small raisins
- 1 red onion
- 2 tablespoons olive oil
- ½ teaspoon cinnamon
- ½ teaspoon ground ginger
- ½ teaspoon ground coriander
- ½ teaspoon turmeric
- ½ teaspoon ground cumin
- ¼ cup toasted slivered almonds
- Handful fresh, flat-leaf parsley
- Handful fresh cilantro

### Preparation

Bring a pan of salted water to a boil and cook the quinoa and currants together for about 15 minutes, or until the quinoa is tender. Drain and set aside to cool slightly.

Peel and finely chop the onion. Warm the oil in a skillet and sauté the onion with the spices for five minutes, until the onion is very soft.

Transfer the quinoa to a large mixing bowl, fluff it up gently with a fork and fold in the cooked onions, almonds, and herbs.

# Five ways with fava beans

## 35

### In their pods

Fava beans can only be eaten in their pods when they are very young, which makes them a real delicacy. Simply top and tail, and eat them raw with a dipping pot of olive oil and balsamic vinegar.

## 36

### Shelled

Once shelled, fava beans have a bright green bean inside a gray-green individual skin. The skins are edible and can be left on for more substantial salads and sides. Boil for two minutes with some fresh peas, then toss with crisp fried onion and fresh herbs. Mint, sage, lemon thyme, and basil are all good.

## 37

### Double-shelled

This involves removing the gray-green outer skin that surrounds each bean. Plunge the beans into boiling water to loosen the skins, pop out the bright green beans and mix into a three-bean salad with kidney beans, chickpeas, and a spicy vinaigrette.

## 38

### Pan-fried

Pan-fry the beans with crushed garlic in a little olive oil or butter—they only need a few moments to warm through. Don't let the garlic brown or the taste will be bitter. Serve over a heap of hot mashed potatoes.

## 39

### Puréed

Blitz leftover beans from the recipes above in a food processor and season generously to make a dip or a flavorsome sandwich filling.

## 40 Zucchini and broccolini tagliatelle

Serves 4

### Ingredients
- 2 zucchini
- ½ pound broccolini
- 1 yellow bell pepper
- 10 ounces tagliatelle
- Handful flat-leaf parsley
- 2 tablespoons olive oil
- Juice ½ lemon
- Salt and freshly ground black pepper

### Preparation

Trim and slice the zucchini into sticks. Trim the broccolini, slicing through any thicker stems. De-seed and finely slice the bell pepper.

Cook the pasta in boiling water until tender. Steam the vegetables for 10 minutes, or until tender—you may be able to save energy by putting the steamer over the pasta pan.

Finely chop half of the parsley and leave the rest whole. Mix the oil, lemon juice and salt and pepper together. To serve, toss the pasta with the warm vegetables, chopped parsley, and dressing. Garnish with the reserved parsley sprigs.

*Broccolini has longer, finer stalks than broccoli, so it is good to eat, but also looks very pretty on the plate. If you can only get curly parsley, use half the quantity and chop it finely. A mixture of green and white tagliatelle with yellow zucchini looks attractive, but don't use black pasta as it is usually colored with squid ink.*

## 41 Stir-fried asparagus with dates and carrots

Serves 4

### Ingredients

- 12 asparagus spears
- 1 inch ginger root
- 3 carrots
- 1 onion
- 6 dates
- 2 tablespoons olive oil
- 1 teaspoon sesame oil
- 4 star anise
- Freshly ground black pepper

### Preparation

Trim the asparagus spears and cut any thick stems in half lengthwise. Peel the ginger and finely chop. Peel the carrots and chop into thin matchsticks. Peel and slice the onion. Roughly chop the dates.

Warm the olive oil and sesame oil together in a large pan or wok. Add the star anise and ginger, and cook for a minute before stirring in the carrot and onion. Stir-fry for four minutes.

Add the asparagus, dates and black pepper and mix well. Stir in 2 tablespoons of water, cover, and cook for five minutes, until the asparagus is tender.

## 42 Authentic falafel

Serves 4

### Ingredients

- 1½ x 15-ounce cans chickpeas
- 1 onion
- 2 cloves garlic
- 4 slices bread
- Few sprigs fresh cilantro
- 1 large egg
- 1¼ cups fresh bread crumbs
- ½ teaspoon dried red pepper flakes
- Salt and freshly ground black pepper
- Canola oil, for the pan

### Preparation

Drain and rinse the chickpeas. Peel and finely chop the onion. Peel and crush the garlic. Tear the bread into pieces. Chop the cilantro. Beat the egg and put the bread crumbs onto a large flat plate.

Place the chickpeas, onion, garlic, torn bread, red pepper flakes, egg, cilantro, and seasoning into the bowl of a food processor and process until smooth.

Divide the mixture into 12 portions. Shape them into patties and roll them in the bread crumbs to coat them.

Heat the oil in a skillet. Flatten the patties with the back of a spoon and fry gently on both sides for about eight minutes, until cooked through and crisp.

*Serve these as they do in the Middle East— inside warmed flat breads such as pita, with salad and tahini sauce or hummus.*

## 43 Vegetable and almond paella

Serves 4

### Ingredients

- 1 onion
- 1 clove garlic
- ½ pound mixed spring vegetables: beans, peas, snow peas, baby zucchini, leeks, scallions, baby carrots
- 1 green bell pepper
- 1 rib celery
- Sprig fresh tarragon
- 2 teaspoons canola oil
- ½ cup blanched almonds
- 1 cup brown rice
- Pinch saffron strands

### Preparation

Peel and finely chop the onion. Peel and crush the garlic. Chop all the remaining vegetables into bite-size pieces. Chop the fresh tarragon.

Warm the oil in a 3-quart pan and sauté the onion for three minutes, then add the garlic and cook gently for a further two minutes. Stir in the almonds and the rice, mix well and cook for a further two minutes, stirring constantly. Add the celery, green bell pepper, mixed vegetables and tarragon, and continue to cook for a further five minutes.

Add 2½ cups boiling water and the saffron strands. Bring to a boil, cover and simmer for 30 minutes until the rice is cooked and the liquid has been absorbed.

*You'll need a large, wide pan with a lid for this Spanish rice dish.*

## 44 Tofu pad thai

Serves 4

### Ingredients

- 14 ounces firm tofu
- ½ cup soy sauce
- ½ pound dried fine rice noodles
- 1 onion
- 4 cloves garlic
- ½ cup peanuts
- 1½ cups bean sproutss
- Juice 1 lemon
- ½ teaspoon sugar
- Dried red pepper flakes, to taste
- 2 tablespoons canola oil

### Preparation

Drain the tofu, cut it into bite-size pieces and put it into a shallow dish with half the soy sauce. Leave to marinate for at least one hour, then gently cook in a dry skillet, turning to seal each side.

Soak the noodles in cold water for 20 minutes. Drain through a colander.

Peel and finely chop the onion. Peel and chop the garlic. Roughly chop the peanuts.

Heat the oil in a wok and sauté the onion and garlic for one minute, then stir in the tofu, noodles, bean sprouts, peanuts, lemon juice, sugar, dried red pepper flakes, and remaining soy sauce. Toss over a high heat for up to three minutes, until heated through.

# 45 Rice noodles with shallots and garlic

Serves 4

### Ingredients

- ½ pound dried fine rice noodles
- 4 shallots
- 4 cloves garlic
- ½ teaspoon sugar
- 1 tablespoon mirin (Japanese rice wine)
- 2 tablespoons soy sauce
- Freshly ground black pepper
- 2 tablespoons canola oil

### Preparation

Soak the noodles in cold water for 20 minutes, then transfer to a colander to drain. Peel and slice the shallots and the garlic. Mix the sugar, mirin, and soy sauce together in a small bowl with a tablespoon of water.

Warm the oil in a wok and sauté the shallots and garlic for a minute, stirring constantly. Add the soy sauce mixture and the noodles, and stir-fry for about three minutes, until the dish is heated through. Season with freshly ground black pepper.

*Rice noodles are popular in the cuisine of Eastern and South-Eastern Asia and are generally only lightly cooked to retain a slightly chewy texture. However, all sorts of noodles are used in East Asian cookery, and although some varieties contain egg and are not suitable for vegans, most are perfect for vegetarian dishes. Mirin has a distinctive sweet-sour flavor and is easy to find in supermarkets and specialty food stores but you can achieve good results with a splash of sweet sherry, or cider vinegar that has been sweetened with a little sugar.*

# Five ways with asparagus

## 46

### Steamed

Put the stalks into a standard steamer over a pan of boiling water, cover, and steam for five minutes (or slightly longer if the stems are very thick). A simple dressing of melted butter or lemon oil is perfect—or go classical with hollandaise sauce (see page 85.)

## 47

### As a salad

Cook the spears for two minutes in boiling water, drain, and toss with vegetarian Parmesan-style cheese, lemon zest, and olive oil. Add a poached egg or some crisp toast to create a complete lunch.

## 48

### Over hot coals

Lay the spears out in a line, aligning the tips and trimming the bases. Push two or three skewers through the row at right angles to secure them, baste with oil and cook each side over hot coals.

## 49

### On the grill

Brush the spears with a little oil and lay them at right angles to the stripes in a grill pan. Try not to move them about too much while they are cooking, so that you'll get the distinctive blackened stripes along the stem, along with a slightly smoky flavor.

## 50

### As a stir-fry

Stir-fry the stems in a little oil for three minutes, then add 3 tablespoons of boiling water. Cover the pan and cook for a further three minutes, until the stems are tender. Serve on rice with crispy fried shallots.

## 51 Mushroom pilaf

Serves 4

### Ingredients

- 1 onion
- 1 red bell pepper
- 4 ounces mixed mushrooms
- Few sprigs fresh parsley
- 1 ½ cups brown rice
- 2 tablespoons olive oil
- 2 ½ cups vegetable bouillon
- 2 tablespoons slivered almonds

### Preparation

Peel and chop the onion. De-seed and chop the red bell pepper. Wipe and slice the mixed mushrooms. Chop the parsley.

Warm the oil in a 3-quart pan and sauté the onion and red bell pepper gently for five minutes, until soft and browning. Stir in the rice, mushrooms, and bouillon. Bring to a boil, cover and simmer for 30 minutes, until the rice is tender and the liquid has been absorbed.

Just before serving, stir in the almonds and parsley.

*You can use whichever mushrooms you prefer for this dish—button, cremini and oyster mushrooms will all work well.*

## 52 Spanish vegetable casserole

Serves 4

### Ingredients

- 1 large onion
- 1 pound baby potatoes
- 3 cloves garlic
- 6 ounces fine green beans
- 1 firm pear
- 1 x 15-ounce can chickpeas
- 2 tablespoons olive oil
- 1 tablespoon paprika
- 1 x 15-ounce can tomatoes, chopped
- 1 ¼ cups vegetable bouillon

### Preparation

Peel and slice the onion. Cut the potatoes into bite-size pieces. Peel and crush the garlic. Trim the beans and chop into short lengths. Core and chop the pear roughly. Drain and rinse the chickpeas.

In a large pan, sauté the onion in the oil for two minutes, then stir in the potatoes, paprika, and garlic. Cook, stirring constantly, for five minutes, then add the beans, pear, tomatoes, chickpeas, and bouillon. Bring to a boil, then simmer, covered, for 30 minutes, until the potatoes are tender.

## 53 Basic crêpes
Makes 6

### Ingredients
- 1 cup all-purpose flour
- Pinch salt
- 1 large egg
- 1 ¼ cups 2% milk
- Canola oil, for the pan

### Preparation
Sift the flour and salt into a large mixing bowl. Make a well in the center. Beat the egg and milk together, then gradually add the wet ingredients to the dry, beating thoroughly to remove any lumps. Alternatively, use a food processor to make a fast, smooth batter.

Heat a little oil in an 8-inch, shallow skillet. Spoon about 2 tablespoons of the batter into the pan and carefully tip the pan so that the batter spreads out evenly. Cook on a high heat for a minute or two, until the bottom of the crêpe is no longer sticky. Turn and cook the other side before sliding onto a warmed plate. Repeat until all of the batter has been used.

*Serve with lemon and sugar, or mix it up with one of the ideas opposite.*

## 54 Ratatouille crêpe filling
Fills 4

### Ingredients
- ½ pound onions
- 2 cloves garlic
- ½ pound zucchini
- 2 red bell peppers
- 1 x 15-ounce can chickpeas
- Few sprigs fresh parsley
- Few sprigs fresh basil
- 1 tablespoon olive oil
- 1 x 15-ounce can tomatoes
- 1 tablespoon sun-dried tomato paste
- Salt and freshly ground black pepper

### Preparation
Peel and roughly chop the onions. Peel and chop the garlic. Trim and slice the zucchini. De-seed and chop the bell peppers. Rinse and drain the chickpeas. Chop the fresh herbs.

Heat the oil in a 3-quart pan and sauté the onions gently for three minutes. Add the garlic and cook for a further minute. Stir in all the remaining ingredients, season, cover and simmer for 30 minutes.

## 55 Soufflé crêpe filling
Fills 4

### Ingredients
- 2 ounces Cheddar cheese
- ½ cup walnuts
- 4 large eggs
- ¼ stick salted butter
- 2 tablespoons all-purpose flour
- ⅔ cup 2% milk
- Salt and freshly ground black pepper

### Preparation
Preheat the oven to 400°F. Shred the cheese and finely chop the walnuts. Beat two of the eggs. Separate the other two eggs into yolks and whites. Add one of the egg yolks to the two beaten eggs and beat again to mix thoroughly. (The remaining egg yolk can be used for another recipe.) Whisk the two egg whites together with a pinch of salt until they form stiff peaks.

Melt the butter in a 3-quart heavy pan. Stir in the flour and cook for a minute, then gradually stir in the milk, keeping the pan on a low heat and beating constantly to prevent lumps as the mixture thickens. Take the pan off the heat and allow the mixture to cool a little. Add the beaten eggs, half the cheese and the seasoning, and beat together well. Transfer the mixture to a large mixing bowl and stir in the walnuts. Finally, gently fold in the beaten egg whites.

Put about 2 tablespoons of the soufflé mixture in a line down the center of each pancake. Carefully fold them up and arrange in a greased baking dish, folded side down. Sprinkle with the remaining cheese and bake for up to 20 minutes, until puffy and bubbling. Serve immediately.

## 56 Crispy chickpea crêpes
Makes 8

### Ingredients
- 2 cups chickpea (gram) flour
- 1 tablespoon garam masala
- 1 teaspoon salt
- Pinch of baking soda
- Few sprigs fresh cilantro
- Canola oil, for the pan

### Preparation
Mix the flour, garam masala, salt, and baking soda together in a large bowl. Gradually add 1¾ cups of water, beating constantly to make a smooth batter. Chop the cilantro and add to the mix.

Heat a little oil in a 10-inch heavy skillet. Spoon 2 to 3 tablespoons of batter into the pan and quickly spread thinly using an oiled spatula. Lightly fry on both sides until crisp at the edges. Serve hot, alongside a dish of curried vegetables or folded around the Curried Baby Potatoes on page 33.

# 57 Walnut and avocado risotto

Serves 4

## Ingredients

- 5 cups warm vegetable bouillon
- 1 onion
- ¼ stick salted butter
- 1½ cups Arborio or other short-grain rice
- ½ cup dry white wine
- 2 ounces vegetarian Parmesan-style cheese
- 2 ripe avocados
- ¾ cup walnut pieces
- Few fresh chives
- Few sprigs fresh parsley

## Preparation

Put the bouillon into a pan and keep it warm on the stove. Peel and finely chop the onion. Melt the butter in a 3-quart heavy pan and gently sauté the onion for five minutes, until soft but not yet beginning to color. Stir the rice into the onions, mix thoroughly and cook for about five minutes, stirring constantly, until the rice begins to look translucent. Pour in the wine and continue to stir until it is absorbed. Then begin to add the bouillon, a little at a time, stirring constantly over a low heat as the bouillon is absorbed. The process should take about 25 minutes and by the time the last of the bouillon is absorbed, the mixture should be thick and the rice tender.

Finely shred the cheese. Peel and dice the avocados. Put the walnut pieces into a dry, heavy pan and heat them gently, stirring frequently, until they begin to color, then turn onto a plate to stop them from cooking further. Chop the chives and parsley.

When the rice is ready, gently stir in the cheese, toasted walnuts and avocado pieces and serve immediately, garnished with the fresh herbs.

*It's important to use a rice such as Arborio or Carnaroli, as these short-grain rices absorb more moisture during cooking and release starch to create the authentic sticky texture of an Italian risotto.*

## 58 Indian-spiced collard greens with coconut

 V

Serves 4

### Ingredients
- 1 pound collard greens
- 2 green chili peppers
- Handful fresh cilantro
- 1 inch ginger root
- Juice ½ lemon
- 1 tablespoon vegetable oil
- 1 teaspoon cumin seeds
- ½ teaspoon black mustard seeds
- ⅔ cup fresh peas
- ½ teaspoon ground coriander
- 2 tablespoons shredded coconut

### Preparation
Wash and shred the collard greens. De-seed the chili peppers and finely chop. Roughly chop the fresh cilantro. Peel and finely chop the ginger.

Warm the oil in a 3-quart pan or wok, and gently toast the cumin seeds, mustard seeds, chopped chili pepper and ginger for two minutes.

Add the greens and the peas, and 2 tablespoons water. Cover the pan and cook on a medium heat for five minutes.

Toss the lemon juice, ground coriander, half of the fresh cilantro and half of the coconut into the greens. Mix well and serve immediately, topped with the remaining fresh cilantro and coconut.

## 59 Spicy coconut rice

Serves 4

 V

### Ingredients
- 1 onion
- 1 red bell pepper
- 1 red chili pepper
- ½ pound broccoli
- 2 tablespoons canola oil
- 2 cups basmati rice
- ⅔ cup coconut milk
- 2½ cups vegetable bouillon
- 1 teaspoon garam masala
- 1 lime
- 2 tablespoons slivered almonds

### Preparation
Peel and roughly chop the onion. De-seed the red bell pepper and cut it into slices. De-seed and finely chop the chili pepper. Cut the broccoli into small florets. Zest and juice the lime.

Heat the oil in a large pan or wok and stir-fry the vegetables for five minutes, until the onion is soft and translucent.

Add the rice, coconut milk and bouillon, stir to combine and bring to a boil. Reduce the heat and simmer very gently, without stirring, for up to 12 minutes, until the rice is cooked. Stir in the garam masala, slivered almonds and lime juice and zest. Heat through and serve immediately.

# 60 Thai stir-fry
Serves 4

## Ingredients
- 1 onion
- 3 cloves garlic
- 1 chili pepper
- 1 inch piece of ginger root
- 1 red bell pepper
- 1 green bell pepper
- 6 scallions
- 4 ounces carrots
- 4 ounces collard greens
- 2 tablespoons soy sauce
- 1 tablespoon tomato paste
- 2 ounces pineapple chunks
- ¾ cup cashew nuts
- 3 tablespoons canola oil
- 4 ounces snow peas

*You can make the first steps of this recipe ahead of time, and then quickly stir-fry once your guests have arrived.*

## Preparation
Peel and slice the onion. Peel and crush the garlic. De-seed and very finely chop the chili pepper. Peel and finely chop the ginger. De-seed the bell peppers and slice them into strips. Trim and chop the scallions. Peel and chop the carrots into thin matchsticks or slices. Wash and shred the greens.

Mix the soy sauce, tomato paste and any juice from the pineapple together in a small bowl or cup. Toast the cashews in a dry, heavy pan for a few minutes until aromatic and browning, then remove from the heat.

Heat the oil in a wok. Add the onion, garlic, chili pepper, and ginger. Stir-fry for one minute,then add the carrots, bell peppers, scallions, and snow peas. Stir-fry for two minutes, then add the pineapple chunks and the collard greens. Stir-fry for a further two minutes and, finally, add the soy sauce and tomato paste mixture and the nuts. Cook for one more minute to warm through and serve immediately.

# 61 Leek quiche

Serves 4

## Ingredients

- ½ pound leeks
- ¼ stick salted butter
- 1 sheet ready-rolled puff pastry
- 6 large eggs
- ½ pound cottage cheese
- Salt and freshly ground black pepper
- Milk, to brush

## Preparation

Preheat the oven to 350°F.

Trim and thinly slice the leeks. Melt the butter in a pan and gently sauté the leeks until they are soft, about seven minutes.

Line a 9-inch quiche or pie pan with the pastry. Use the pastry trimmings to cut leaf shapes to decorate the edge of the quiche later.

Beat the eggs and cottage cheese together and season with salt and pepper. Stir in the cooked leeks, mix well and pour into the prepared quiche base. Decorate with the pastry leaves and brush with a little milk. Bake for up to 30 minutes, until the quiche is cooked through and the pie crust is golden.

*Leeks are a traditional filling for the traditional French quiche, but here they are mixed with cottage cheese, which is lower in fat than hard cheeses like Cheddar.*

# 62 Macaroni cheese with fennel

Serves 4

## Ingredients
- 1 bulb fennel
- 2 ounces Cheddar cheese
- Few fresh chives
- 1 onion
- 1 ½ cups 2% milk
- 1 bay leaf
- 6 ounces whole-wheat macaroni
- 3 tablespoons salted butter
- 2 tablespoons all-purpose flour
- Freshly ground black pepper

*This is my take on a traditional mac and cheese, which uses less cheese—so it is healthier, but just as tasty and comforting!*

## Preparation
Preheat the oven to 375°F.

Roughly chop the fennel, reserving any fronds for a garnish. Shred the cheese. Chop the fresh chives.

Peel the onion and cut it in half. Put it into a 1 ½-quart pan with the milk and bay leaf. Bring to a boil, then remove from the heat and let stand for 15 minutes. Then remove and discard the onion and bay leaf.

Bring a 3-quart pan of salted water to a boil and cook the macaroni until just tender. Drain and set aside.

Melt the butter in a heavy pan. Stir in the flour and cook for a minute before gradually adding the milk. Keep beating the mixture to prevent any lumps from forming. Bring the sauce to a boil, stirring continuously as it thickens. When the sauce has thickened, reduce the heat to a bare simmer, add half of the shredded cheese and stir well to mix. When the cheese has melted into the sauce, stir in the macaroni, fennel, and black pepper.

Transfer the mixture to a baking dish, top with the remaining cheese and bake for 25 minutes, until golden and bubbling. Sprinkle with fresh chopped chives and garnish with fennel fronds just before serving.

# 63 Mushroom and tomato spaghetti casserole

Serves 4

## Ingredients

- 4 ounces button mushrooms
- 1 onion
- 1 clove garlic
- Few sprigs fresh oregano
- ½ pound whole-wheat spaghetti
- 2 teaspoons olive oil
- 1 x 15-ounce can diced tomatoes
- 1 tablespoon sun-dried tomato paste
- 2 ounces Cheddar cheese

## Preparation

Preheat the oven to 350°F.

Wipe and slice the mushrooms. Peel and roughly chop the onion and garlic. Chop the fresh oregano.

Bring a 3-quart pan of salted water to a boil and cook the spaghetti until tender. Drain and set aside.

Heat the oil in a pan and gently sauté the onion for three minutes. Add the garlic and cook for a further minute or two. Stir in the mushrooms and cook, covered, for five more minutes. Add the canned tomatoes, tomato paste, and oregano and simmer gently for 10 minutes.

Mix the sauce into the spaghetti thoroughly and transfer to a baking dish. Shred the Cheddar cheese and sprinkle over the spaghetti. Bake for 25 minutes, until golden and bubbling.

*Whole-wheat spaghetti is a must for this dish, as it has a distinctive texture and will not turn to mush during cooking.*

# 64 Asparagus tagliatelle

Serves 4

### Ingredients
- 1 pound asparagus
- 14 ounces fresh tagliatelle
- Small handful fresh, flat-leaf parsley
- Few sprigs fresh dill
- Few sprigs fresh chives
- 3 tablespoons lemon oil
- 1 tablespoon sea salt flakes

### Preparation

Cut the asparagus into short pieces—using just the tips is prettiest for this dish, but you can use the stems too, or reserve them for another dish. Prepare a 3-quart pan of boiling salted water, with a steamer on top. Cook the pasta in the water, and at the same time, steam the asparagus tips. Both the pasta and the asparagus tips should be ready in around five minutes. While cooking, chop the herbs.

Drain the pasta and arrange it on four serving plates, topped with the asparagus, chopped herbs, lemon oil and a sprinkle of sea salt flakes, to taste.

*Tagliatelle are long flat ribbons of pasta, which are sometimes colored with spinach or tomato. They are often sold dried in small "nests"— take care to loosen them when cooking in boiling water, so that they cook evenly.*

# 65 Spaghetti with lemon and parsley

Serves 4

## Ingredients
- 3 ounces vegetarian Parmesan-style cheese
- Small handful fresh parsley
- 10 ounces spaghetti
- ¼ stick salted butter
- Zest 1 lemon
- Freshly ground black pepper

## Preparation
Shred the cheese finely and chop the parsley. Bring a 3-quart pan of salted water to a boil and cook the spaghetti until tender. Drain and toss with the butter, cheese, parsley, lemon zest, and black pepper. Serve immediately.

*This simple dish will become a family favorite—fresh lemon zest and parsley bring the flavors to life. Traditional Parmesan and Grana Padano cheeses are made with animal rennet so look for a hard cheese that is labeled "suitable for vegetarians."*

# 66 Spring vegetables with tarragon mayonnaise

Serves 4

### Ingredients

- 4 ounces broccoli
- 4 ounces baby carrots
- 4 ounces sugar snap peas
- 4 ounces snow peas
- 4 ounces zucchini
- 4 ounces fresh peas

### For the mayonnaise

- 4 large eggs
- Small handful fresh tarragon
- 2 teaspoons mild mustard
- 1 tablespoon white wine vinegar
- 2 ½ cups vegetable oil
- Salt and freshly ground white pepper

### Preparation

Cut the broccoli into small florets and halve any thick carrots. Steam the broccoli, carrots, sugar snap peas, and snow peas for 10 minutes, until just tender. Thinly slice the zucchini.

Make the mayonnaise. Separate the egg yolks from the whites (save the whites for another dish). Finely chop the tarragon.

Put the egg yolks into a blender with the mustard and vinegar. Switch the machine on and gradually pour in the oil. The mixture should emulsify and thicken as you watch. Spoon the mayonnaise out of the blender and transfer to a small mixing bowl. Stir in the chopped tarragon and season to taste with salt and pepper.

Serve the steamed vegetables, along with the raw peas and zucchini slices, arranged on a plate with a little pot of mayonnaise, or mix all the vegetables together in a large bowl and toss the mayonnaise through immediately before serving.

# Five ways with artichokes

## 67

### Steamed

Cut off the stalks and boil standing up in a 3-quart pan with a splash of salt and lemon. Cover and cook for 40 minutes or until a leaf can easily be pulled off. Turn out upside down to drain and set aside. They are best served tepid. Mix mustard and wine vinegar with olive oil, season with salt and sugar, and serve as a dip.

## 68

### Sautéed

Prepare and cook artichokes as above, then sauté the hearts (one per person) with mushrooms. Dress with sherry vinegar. Serve with baby romaine salad and cherry tomatoes.

## 69

### Broiled

Prepare and cook artichokes as above, then cut them in half lengthwise; remove the choke, brush with oil and broil until lightly charred. Serve with the dressing from recipe 67, with added honey.

## 70

### Roasted

Prepare the artichokes as above but do not boil them. Cut them into halves and remove the choke. Drizzle with oil and a squeeze of lemon and roast in the oven at 400°F for about 40 minutes.

## 71

### Stuffed

Prepare the artichoke as above but do not boil them. Fill the center with a mixture of bread crumbs, vegetarian Parmesan-style cheese, garlic, and herbs of your choice, and steam gently.

# 72 Oriental omelet parcels

Serves 4

## Ingredients

- 3 large eggs
- 1 tablespoon mirin (Japanese rice wine)
- 1 teaspoon toasted sesame oil
- Vegetable oil, for the pan
- Salt and freshly ground black pepper

## For the filling

- 1 cup bean sprouts
- 3 scallions
- 1 carrot
- 2 radishes
- 1 tablespoon toasted sesame oil
- 1 tablespoon soy sauce

## Preparation

Break the eggs into a bowl and beat together well with the mirin and sesame oil. Season to taste with salt and black pepper. Heat a little oil in an 8-inch skillet and use the mixture to make four thin omelets. Interleave the omelets with parchment paper and keep in the oven on a very low heat while you prepare the filling.

Trim and finely slice the scallions. Shred the carrot and radishes. Warm the sesame oil in a wok and stir-fry the vegetables for one minute, until heated through but still crisp. Splash the soy sauce into the warm mixture and toss through.

Divide the warm stir-fried mixture between the omelets and fold like parcels to serve.

*Japanese rice wine (mirin) adds a sweetness to these omelets, while toasted sesame oil has a distinctive nutty flavor that works well with all kinds of stir-fried vegetable dishes.*

# 73 Leek risotto torte

Serves 4

### Ingredients
- 1 pound leeks
- 1 onion
- 3 cloves garlic
- Small handful fresh basil
- ½ stick salted butter
- 1 cup Arborio rice
- ¾ cup dry white wine
- 2 cups warm vegetable bouillon
- 2 large eggs
- ¼ cup crème fraîche or sour cream
- 4 ounces vegetarian Parmesan-style cheese
- Salt and freshly ground black pepper

### Preparation

Trim and finely slice the leeks. Peel and chop the onion. Peel and chop the garlic. Chop the fresh basil. Melt the butter in a 3-quart pan and gently sauté the leeks, onion, and garlic for two minutes. Stir in the rice and cook for a further two minutes until the rice starts to become translucent. Add the wine and cook, stirring constantly, until it has been absorbed by the rice.

Add the bouillon a little at a time, stirring constantly, allowing it to be absorbed by the rice. Adding all the bouillon will take about 25 minutes and then the rice will be cooked and thickened.

Preheat the oven to 400°F and grease and line a 9-inch round cake pan.

Beat the eggs and mix them into the risotto with the fresh basil, crème fraîche, cheese, and seasoning. Spoon into the pan, smooth the top and bake for up to 25 minutes, until firm and golden. Let cool slightly before turning out of the pan and slicing.

# 74 Turkish turlu turlu

Serves 4

### Ingredients

- 1 eggplant
- 4 ounces okra
- 10 ounces green beans
- 2 onions
- 1 green bell pepper
- 4 zucchini
- 14 ounces potatoes
- 4 to 5 fresh tomatoes
- Large handful fresh parsley
- 9 ounces peas
- 1 x 15-ounce can tomatoes
- ⅓ cup olive oil
- Salt and freshly ground black pepper
- 2 teaspoons paprika

### Preparation

Preheat the oven to 375°F.

Cut the eggplant into cubes, put in a colander and sprinkle with salt. Leave for 30 minutes, then rinse and pat dry with paper towels.

Trim the okra, removing the stalks, and trim the beans. Peel and roughly chop the onions. De-seed and roughly chop the bell pepper. Trim and slice the zucchini. Peel the potatoes and chop into bite-size chunks. Slice the fresh tomatoes. Chop the parsley.

Put the prepared eggplant, okra, peas, beans, zucchini, onions, potatoes, bell peppers, parsley, and canned tomatoes in a casserole dish. Pour over ¼ cup olive oil, season with salt, pepper, and paprika and mix together thoroughly. Smooth out the top of the mixture and cover with slices of tomato. Finish with the remaining olive oil.

Bake for 60 minutes, until the tomatoes are starting to brown. Serve with fresh bread.

# 75 Thai green curry

Serves 4

**For the curry paste**

- 1 stalk lemongrass
- 2 to 3 green chili peppers, to taste
- 2 inch ginger root
- 4 to 5 cloves garlic
- 1 shallot
- Large handful fresh cilantro
- 3 kaffir lime leaves, optional
- $\frac{1}{3}$ cup coconut milk
- 1 tablespoon soy sauce
- 2 tablespoons lime juice
- 1 tablespoon sugar
- $\frac{1}{2}$ teaspoon ground cumin
- $\frac{1}{2}$ teaspoon ground coriander
- Salt and freshly ground white pepper to taste

**For the curry**

- Vegetable oil, for stir-frying
- 1 x 15-ounce can chickpeas
- 1 cup vegetable bouillon
- 1 green or red bell pepper
- 1 eggplant, or 4 Thai eggplants
- 1 $\frac{1}{2}$ cups coconut milk
- 7 ounces firm tofu
- 4 ounces sliced bamboo shoots

**Preparation**

Make the curry paste first. Trim and finely slice the lemongrass. De-seed and chop the chili peppers, peel and slice the ginger, garlic, and shallot, and chop the cilantro. Put all the curry paste ingredients into a food processor and blend until smooth.

Chop the vegetables into bite-size pieces. Warm the vegetable oil in a wok and add the curry paste. Heat it through, stirring constantly, for one minute, then add the drained, rinsed chickpeas, vegetable bouillon, and eggplant and simmer for five minutes. Drain and pat dry the tofu and cut into strips. Stir in the pepper, tofu, and bamboo shoots and cook gently for a few minutes. When the vegetables are softened but still quite firm, stir in the coconut milk and heat through. Serve immediately, garnished with fresh herbs.

# 76 Beans bourguignon

Serves 4

## Ingredients

- 1 onion
- 2 cloves garlic
- 1 large carrot
- 1 large potato
- ½ pound mushrooms
- 2 tablespoons olive oil
- 3 tablespoons tomato paste
- 1 teaspoon dried thyme
- 2 bay leaves
- 1 x 15-ounce can navy beans
- 1½ cups red wine
- ¼ stick salted butter
- Salt and freshly ground black pepper

## Preparation

Peel and chop the onion. Peel and crush the garlic. Peel the carrot and potato. Chop the carrot into thin slices and the potato into small cubes. Wipe and slice the mushrooms.

Warm the olive oil in a flameproof casserole dish and sauté the onion for three minutes. Stir in the potato and carrot. Add 1 cup of water. Stir in the tomato paste, thyme, and bay leaves. Bring to a boil and cook for 15 minutes. Add the beans, wine, and garlic. Turn the heat down and simmer gently for a further 10 minutes. Remove the bay leaves.

Melt the butter in a skillet and gently sauté the mushrooms for up to three minutes. Stir them into the beans and adjust seasoning with salt and pepper before serving.

*A tasty classic French sauce made with herbs and red wine makes an inexpensive dish of beans into a more sophisticated offering!*

## 77 Vegetable casserole with apricots

Serves 4

 **V**

### Ingredients

- 1 onion
- 2 cloves garlic
- 1 head celery
- 3 zucchini
- 1 yellow bell pepper
- 1 green bell pepper
- 12 dried apricots
- 3 tablespoons olive oil
- 1 teaspoon turmeric
- 1 bay leaf
- 1 x 15-ounce can diced tomatoes
- 1 x 15-ounce can chickpeas
- 1½ cups vegetable bouillon
- Pinch cayenne pepper
- Salt and freshly ground black pepper

### Preparation

Peel and roughly chop the onion. Peel and crush the garlic. Trim and roughly chop the celery, zucchini, and peppers. Chop the apricots into quarters.

Warm the oil in a large flameproof casserole dish and gently sauté the onion, garlic, celery, peppers, turmeric, and bay leaf for five minutes. Add the apricots, tomatoes, chickpeas, and bouillon; cover and simmer for 30 minutes. Season to taste with cayenne, salt, and pepper.

## 78 Mexican chickpeas with paprika

Serves 4

 **V**

### Ingredients

- 3 onions
- 4 cloves garlic
- ¼ cup olive oil
- 1 teaspoon cayenne pepper
- 2 teaspoons ground coriander
- 2 teaspoons ground cumin
- 2 teaspoons paprika
- 1 teaspoon turmeric
- 1 pound dried chickpeas
- 2 cups vegetable bouillon
- 1 x 15-ounce can diced tomatoes
- 2 tablespoons tomato paste

### Preparation

Peel and roughly chop the onions. Peel and crush the garlic. Gently sauté the onion and garlic in the oil for five minutes in a 3-quart pan until the onion is soft. Stir in the cayenne, coriander, cumin, paprika, and turmeric and cook for a further minute before adding the chickpeas, bouillon, tomatoes, and tomato paste. Bring to a boil, then reduce the heat, cover, and simmer for one hour, until the chickpeas are cooked. This dish can be served hot or cold.

*If using canned chickpeas, cook for 15 minutes rather than the full hour.*

## 79 Spicy bean casserole

Serves 4

### Ingredients
- 1 onion
- 1 clove garlic
- 1 zucchini
- 1 red or green bell pepper
- 1 x 15-ounce can navy beans
- 1 x 15-ounce can red kidney beans
- 2 tablespoons olive oil
- 2 tablespoons all-purpose flour
- 1 teaspoon mild chili powder
- 1 x 15-ounce can diced tomatoes
- 1 teaspoon sun-dried tomato paste
- ⅔ cup vegetable bouillon
- ⅔ cup corn
- Salt and freshly ground black pepper

### Preparation
Peel and roughly chop the onion. Peel and crush the garlic. Trim and slice the zucchini. De-seed and slice the bell pepper. Drain and rinse the canned beans.

Gently sauté the onion and garlic in the oil for five minutes, until soft. Stir in the flour, chili powder, canned tomatoes, and tomato paste, then gradually add the bouillon, stirring to prevent any lumps from forming. Add the zucchini, peppers, beans, and corn and bring to a boil. Reduce the heat and simmer, covered, for 10 minutes, until the zucchini is tender.

Season to taste and serve hot.

## 80 Easy-baked brown rice

Serves 4

### Ingredients
- 2 onions
- 3 cloves garlic
- 1 inch ginger root
- 4 cardamom pods
- 1 cinnamon stick
- 2 tablespoons canola oil
- 1 teaspoon cumin seeds
- 1 teaspoon coriander seeds
- 1 ⅓ cups brown long-grain rice
- 2 cups vegetable bouillon
- Handful fresh, chopped cilantro

### Preparation
Preheat oven to 300°F.

Peel and thinly slice the onions. Peel and slice the garlic. Shred the ginger. Lightly crush the cardamom pods and cinnamon stick.

Put the onion, garlic, ginger, and oil into a flameproof casserole dish and sauté gently for two minutes. Add all the remaining ingredients except the cilantro. Stir to mix, then cover with a lid or aluminum foil and bake in the oven for one hour. Garnish with the cilantro to serve.

# Five ways with peas

## 81

### Straight from the garden

There is no need to cook freshly picked peas. Enjoy them raw as part of a fresh salad. Their sweetness contrasts well with the earthy taste of baby beets and the lemony tang of feta cheese.

## 82

### Pea shoots

A pretty and versatile addition to salads, pea shoots are easy to grow, even if you don't have a garden. Simply plant whole dried peas in shallow trays, water regularly and watch them shoot up. Harvest when they are about 3 inches tall, before they start to tangle together.

## 83

### Pea purée

Purée fresh peas with fresh mint and a little melted butter, and serve as a side dish. Or you can blend lemon juice, black pepper, bread crumbs and vegetarian ricotta cheese for a smooth pâté.

## 84

### Cocktail fritters

Stir into a thick, well-seasoned batter and deep-fry to make bite-size cocktail snacks, perfect for the year's first outdoor gatherings.

## 85

### Pea shooters

Make a light pea and mint soup, chill in the refrigerator, and add a splash of lemon vodka. Serve as an appetizer in chilled shot glasses garnished with fresh pea shoots.

## 86 Spring fling
Serves 4

### Ingredients
- Half cucumber
- 3 lemons
- Handful fresh mint
- 1 cup vodka
- 3–4 tablespoons white sugar, to taste
- 1 cup sparkling mineral water

### Preparation
Thinly slice the cucumber and one of the lemons. Juice the remaining lemons. Chop the mint roughly.

Put the cucumber and lemon slices, lemon juice, vodka, mint, and sugar in a large jug. Cover and chill for 30 minutes.

Stir the mixture to help dissolve the sugar and chill for a further 30 minutes. Add the water and serve over ice in long glasses.

## 87 Fruit cooler
Serves 4

### Ingredients
- 1¾ cups pineapple juice
- 1¾ cups orange juice
- 1¾ cups grapefruit juice
- ½ cup grenadine syrup

### Preparation
Mix all the ingredients together in a big jug with lots of ice!

## 88 Rhubarb and ginger cordial

Serves 4

### Ingredients
- 10 ounces rhubarb
- 2 inch piece of ginger root
- Juice 1 lemon
- 1 orange
- 1 ¼ cups sugar

### Preparation

Trim the rhubarb and cut it into
1-inch pieces. Peel and roughly
chop the ginger. Zest and juice
the orange.

Put the sugar, rhubarb, lemon juice,
orange zest and juice, and ginger into
a large pan with 1 ½ cups of water. Warm
the pan to dissolve the sugar, then bring
to a boil. Boil for five minutes, then
remove from the heat and let cool. Strain
through a cheesecloth and store in a
sterilized bottle in the refrigerator. Serve
mixed with sparkling mineral water.

## 89 Spring tonic smoothie

Serves 4

### Ingredients
- 1 large ripe banana
- 3 ounces spinach
- ½ cup blueberries
- ½ cup strawberries
- 2 cups cold 2% milk
  or non-dairy alternative

### Preparation

Peel and chop the banana. Shred the
spinach. Blend all the ingredients together
in a blender or food processor.

## 90 Rhubarb and mascarpone phyllo purses

Serves 4

### Ingredients

- 2 tablespoons stem ginger in syrup
- ½ pound mascarpone cheese
- 2 tablespoons unsweetened shredded coconut
- 1 rib rhubarb
- 3 tablespoons salted butter
- 3 sheets phyllo pastry
- 2 tablespoons sugar

### For the coulis

- 1 rib rhubarb
- 4 ounces ripe strawberries
- 4 ounces sugar

### Preparation

Preheat the oven to 400°F.

Chop the ginger finely and mix it into the mascarpone. Add the coconut and mix well. Trim the rhubarb and slice into pieces no more than ½ inch thick.

Melt the butter and brush half of it over one sheet of pastry. Cover with a second sheet of pastry, brush with butter and top with the third pastry sheet. Use a sharp knife to cut the pastry into four equal squares, working quickly so that the pastry doesn't dry out. Divide the mascarpone mixture between the pastry pieces, press in some of the rhubarb, and finish with sugar. Bring the corners of the pastry up and squeeze together to seal into a purse shape. Transfer to a parchment paper-lined baking sheet and bake for 10 minutes, until the pastry is golden.

To make the coulis, trim and finely chop the rhubarb. Finely chop the strawberries. Place the fruit into a 1½-quart pan with the sugar and cook gently for 10 minutes, until the sugar has dissolved and the fruit is meltingly soft. Pass the mixture through a sieve. Spoon a pool of the coulis onto a serving plate and place the phyllo purse on top. Serve immediately.

*Mascarpone is a smooth Italian cream cheese that can be used for sweet or savory dishes.*

## 91 Classic lemon tart
Serves 8

### Ingredients
- ¾ stick unsalted butter
- 1 ½ cups all-purpose flour
- 1 tablespoon confectioners' sugar
- 1 large egg yolk

### For the filling
- Juice 3 lemons
- 2 tablespoons cornstarch
- 3 large egg yolks
- ½ cup sugar
- ⅔ cup heavy cream
- Zest 1 lemon

### Preparation
Cut the butter into small pieces and blend it into the flour with your fingertips. Stir in the confectioners' sugar and the egg yolk and mix well. Gradually add cold water, a splash at a time, until the dough comes together and is soft but not sticky. Gather into a ball, wrap in a plastic food bag and chill for 20 minutes.

Preheat the oven to 375°F. Roll the pastry out thinly and line an 8- to 9-inch fluted pie pan. Prick the base and let "rest" for a further 20 minutes. Then line the base with parchment paper and fill with baking beans.

Bake for 15 minutes, then remove the beans and paper and return to the oven for five more minutes. Set aside. Turn the oven temperature down to 350°F.

To make the filling, add enough cold water to the lemon juice to make 2 cups. Transfer to a small pan and beat in the cornstarch. Turn on the heat and gradually bring the mixture to a boil, stirring constantly. When the consistency is like a thick sauce, take the pan off the heat and let the mixture cool. Beat in the egg yolks, sugar, cream, and lemon zest, and return the pan to the heat. Gradually bring to a boil, stirring constantly. As soon as it begins to bubble, pour it into the pastry crust and bake for 20 minutes. Cool and chill thoroughly before slicing.

## 92 Lattice-topped custard tart

Serves 6

### Ingredients
- 1 stick plus 1 tablespoon cold unsalted butter
- 1 ½ cups all-purpose flour
- ¼ cup sugar
- 1 large egg yolk
- 2 tablespoons raspberry preserve

### For the filling
- 2 large eggs plus 1 egg yolk
- 1 ½ cups 2% milk
- 2 tablespoons granulated brown sugar
- ½ teaspoon ground nutmeg
- 1 tablespoon pine nuts
- Milk for glazing
- Confectioners' sugar, to serve

### Preparation

Preheat the oven to 400°F. Cut the butter into small pieces and blend it into the flour using your fingertips. Stir in the sugar and then mix in the egg yolk. If the dough doesn't come together, add a splash of water. Turn onto a floured surface and knead for about three minutes, until smooth. Wrap in a plastic food bag and chill for 30 minutes.

Roll the pastry out thinly and line a deep, 8-inch pie pan. Save the trimmings for later. Refrigerate the pastry shell for a further 10 minutes, then line it with parchment paper and fill it with baking beans. Bake for 10 minutes, then remove the beans and parchment and bake for a further six minutes or so until it begins to color. Set aside and turn the oven down to 350°F. When the pastry shell has cooled a little, brush the base with raspberry preserve.

To make the custard, whisk the eggs, egg yolk, milk, sugar, and nutmeg together. Pour into the pastry shell and bake for 25 minutes. Re-roll the pastry trimmings, then cut into long strips approximately 1-inch wide. Remove the tart from the oven and arrange the strips in a lattice over the top. Sprinkle with pine nuts, brush with a little milk and return to the oven for a further 20 minutes until just set. Dust with confectioners' sugar before serving.

# Summer

## Soups, salads, and appetizers

## Mains and sides

## Drinks and sweets

# Fresh in Season ...

### Tomatoes

The quintessential summer food—they are never as good at any other time of year, and are best still warm from the sun. Look out for yellow and orange tomatoes and interesting heritage varieties. Simply slice, top with quality olive oil and basil, and serve with good bread.

### Zucchini

Zucchini should be dark green and glossy, with no soft spots. Baby zucchini are a seasonal delicacy—quarter them lengthwise and serve raw with an aioli dip. Larger specimens are great halved and grilled on the barbecue.

### New season baby potatoes

Baby new potatoes are a summer treat, making a salad into a satisfying meal. Choose small, regular sized potatoes with flaking, papery skins and scrub them (no need to peel). Top with good salted butter or a dollop of vegan mayonnaise.

### Eggplants

Eggplants should be firm and smooth, with a uniform dark colour. They're a barbecue favorite—grill until the skins are black, scoop out the soft flesh and mash with tahini and minced garlic to make a dip that's great hot or cold.

### Radishes

Too often confined to the salad bowl, radishes add delicious fresh peppery flavor to sandwiches, picnics, and stir-fries. For a stylish appetizer, serve small radishes whole, with olive oil and sea salt to dip into.

### Avocados

Choose avocados that are neither rock hard nor too soft. If they ripen more before you are ready to eat them, mash them into a guacamole. Firm avocados can be halved, destoned, filled with a savory nut mixture and baked.

### Cucumbers

Cucumbers should be dark green and very firm. Keep them in the refrigerator and if they are wrapped in plastic, leave it on to maximize shelf life. Cold slices of cucumber are great for quickly cooling tall summer drinks.

### Peppers

Like cucumbers, tomatoes, and zucchini, these summer veggies are strictly fruits! Try adding crisp, chilled slices to colorful summer salads or stuff them, wrap them in foil and bake or barbecue until soft and juicy.

## 93 Mango and sunflower seed pâté

Serves 4

### Ingredients
- 1 cup sunflower seeds
- 1 ripe mango
- ½ jalapeño pepper
- 1 clove garlic
- 1 tablespoon soy sauce
- Juice ½ lime
- 1 scallion

### Preparation

Cover the sunflower seeds with water and soak for eight hours or overnight. Drain and rinse them.

Peel, pit, and finely chop the mango. De-seed and finely chop the jalapeño pepper. Peel and crush the garlic. Finely chop the scallion. Put the seeds into a food processor with the jalapeño, garlic, soy sauce, and lime juice, and pulse until smooth. Transfer to a bowl and mix in the mango and chopped scallion. Serve chilled with crackers or crusty bread.

## 94 New season baby potato salad

Serves 4

### Ingredients
- 1 clove garlic
- ½ pound baby new season potatoes
- ¼ stick salted butter
- 4 ounces fresh watercress
- 2 teaspoons balsamic vinegar

### Preparation

Peel and crush the garlic. Boil the potatoes in salted water until tender. Drain and thickly slice. Return to the warm pan along with the butter and garlic, and toss together to melt the butter. Cool to room temperature and then refrigerate for at least an hour so that the butter sets. Trim the watercress and chop it into short lengths. To serve, toss the potatoes with the watercress and balsamic vinegar.

*To make this feature salad, you should look out for the first crop of baby potatoes to arrive in the store.*

## 95 Spanish watermelon soup

Serves 4

### Ingredients

- 1 ¾ pounds ripe, seedless watermelon
- 4 tomatoes
- 1 clove garlic
- 3 slices white bread
- ⅓ cup toasted slivered almonds
- 2 tablespoons olive oil
- 2 tablespoons red wine vinegar
- ½ teaspoon paprika
- ½ teaspoon ground cumin
- Salt and freshly ground black pepper

### Preparation

Roughly chop the watermelon. Peel and chop the tomatoes. Peel and crush the garlic. Put the bread onto a plate and cover with water—allow to soak for five minutes, then squeeze the bread to remove excess moisture.

Put the bread into the bowl of a food processor with the tomatoes, almonds, olive oil, vinegar, garlic, paprika, and cumin. Process until smooth, then add the watermelon and process again. Strain the mixture through a fine sieve, season to taste and chill thoroughly before serving.

*This refreshing chilled soup is thickened with bread and almonds which makes it a light but satisfying summertime meal.*

## 96 Chunky gazpacho

Serves 4

### Ingredients

- 3 large ripe tomatoes
- 2 ripe avocados
- 1 small red onion
- 1 green chili pepper
- 1 clove garlic
- Handful fresh cilantro
- Handful fresh parsley
- Handful fresh basil
- Juice 1 lime
- Salt and freshly ground black pepper
- Ice cubes, to serve

### Preparation

Roughly chop the tomatoes. Peel, pit, and chop the avocados. Peel and chop the onion. Peel and chop the garlic. De-seed and finely chop the chili pepper. Chop the herbs. Put all of the ingredients into the bowl of a food processor and pulse to combine. You are aiming for a chunky consistency, not a purée. Season to taste with salt and pepper. Chill for an hour and top each serving with a cube or two of ice.

# Five ways with cucumber

## 97

### Sandwiches

Cut the cucumber lengthwise, scoop out the seeds and finely slice. Sprinkle with salt and leave in a colander for 30 minutes. Rinse under ice-cold water, pat dry and sandwich between thinly sliced, buttered white bread, with the crusts cut off.

## 98

### Soups

Slice and sauté cucumber with garlic and onions, then purée. Loosen with vegetable bouillon, white wine, and cream, then flavor to taste with fresh herb—mint is a favorite.

## 99

### Cocktails

Flavor gin or vodka by putting peeled, de-seeded and chopped cucumber into a large jar, covering with alcohol, sealing and leaving to steep for a week. Strain, and use to make cocktails.

## 100

### Raita

Cucumber raita is a cooling Indian dip made from shredded cucumber and plain yogurt, often with finely chopped mint or fresh green chili pepper. Serve with hot and spicy foods such as chilies, tagines, Mexican dishes, and spicy barbecues.

## 101

### Stir-fries

Cucumber is rarely served cooked, but this works well in Asian menus. Slice into very fine ribbons and stir-fry for two minutes with a little soy sauce, garlic, and toasted sesame oil. Serve as a side dish or in place of noodles.

# 102 Asparagus spears with hollandaise sauce

Serves 4

## Ingredients
- 1 bunch asparagus
- 1 tablespoon vegetable oil

## For the sauce
- 2 tablespoons lemon juice
- ¾ cup nonfat milk
- 1 tablespoon salted butter
- 1 teaspoon cornstarch
- Salt and freshly ground black pepper
- 1 large egg

## Preparation
Bend the asparagus stems until they snap naturally. Discard the lower woody ends. Bring a 3-quart pan of salted water to a boil. Plunge the asparagus into the water, cook for around three minutes, then drain. Arrange immediately on a plate, or toss with a little vegetable oil and cook in a hot grill pan, until the asparagus spears are marked with deep brown lines.

To make the hollandaise sauce, mix half the lemon juice with the milk. Melt the butter in a small pan, cook for a minute until it is golden, then pour into a small bowl and set aside.

Put ¼ cup of the milk and lemon mixture into a small bowl or cup and mix in the cornstarch, salt, and pepper, stirring well to prevent any lumps from forming. Warm the remaining milk in a heavy pan, and gradually add the cornstarch mixture and the egg, beating continuously. Continue to cook the sauce over a medium heat until it reaches simmering point. Remove from the heat and beat in the remaining lemon juice and the melted butter. Serve immediately with the asparagus.

## 103 Fava bean and mozzarella bruschetta

Serves 4

### Ingredients

- ½ pound shelled fava beans
- 3 tablespoons olive oil
- Juice 1 lemon
- Handful fresh mint
- Salt and freshly ground black pepper
- 4 slices crusty bread
- 1 clove garlic
- 5 ounces mozzarella cheese

### Preparation

Bring a pan of salted water to a boil. Plunge the beans into the boiling water, cook for two minutes and, using a slotted spoon, scoop them out of the hot water and into a bowl of cold water. Peel away and discard the skins. Roughly crush the beans with the olive oil and lemon juice. Chop the mint and mix into the paste. Season with salt and pepper.

Toast the bread. Peel the garlic, then rub the crisp surface of the toasted bread with the whole clove of garlic. Top each slice of bread with the bean mixture, tear the mozzarella into small pieces and scatter over the bruschetta.

*Fava beans look so much more alluring when you take the time to pop them out of their skins! They make a purée that is smoother and more colorful too.*

## 104 Minted lettuce soup

Serves 4

### Ingredients

- 4 shallots
- 1 clove garlic
- ½ pound baby potatoes
- 1 baby romaine lettuce
- Small handful fresh mint
- ¼ stick salted butter
- 1 quart vegetable bouillon
- ¾ cup fresh or frozen peas
- Salt and freshly ground black pepper
- ⅔ cup half and half

### Preparation

Peel and finely chop the shallots. Peel and crush the garlic. Finely slice the potatoes. Shred the lettuce and chop the mint.

Melt the butter in a 3-quart pan and gently cook the shallots until soft and translucent. Add the garlic and cook for another minute, then stir in the potatoes and bouillon. Bring to a boil, reduce the heat and simmer, covered, until the potatoes are falling apart, around 15 minutes. Add the lettuce, mint, and peas and cook for five more minutes, then take off the heat and let cool.

Transfer to a food processor and blend until smooth. Season to taste with salt and pepper, and chill. Swirl the half and half into the cold soup just before serving.

## 105 Summer day salad

Serves 4

### Ingredients

- 1 mango
- 1 avocado
- 2 carrots
- 6 scallions
- 1 clove garlic
- 1 inch ginger root
- 2 tablespoons canola oil
- 2 tablespoons lime juice
- Seeds of ½ pomegranate
- Salt and freshly ground black pepper

### Preparation

Peel, pit and slice the mango and the avocado. Peel the carrots, if necessary, and slice as thinly as possible. Trim and slice the scallions. Peel and crush the garlic. Peel and shred the ginger. Combine the oil and lime juice and mix in the shredded ginger and garlic. Put all the ingredients into a large serving bowl and toss well to combine. Season and serve immediately.

*Pomegranate seeds are so beautiful— they add a splash of color to all sorts of dishes. Simply cut the fruit in half and delve with your fingers to free them from the white pith.*

## 106 Mushroom, arugula, and red kidney bean salad

Serves 4

### Ingredients
- 1 cup canned red kidney beans
- 1 red onion
- 4 ounces button mushrooms
- 2 ounces arugula

### For the dressing
- 1 tablespoon soy sauce
- 2 tablespoons olive oil
- Juice 1 lemon
- 1 teaspoon honey
- Salt and freshly ground black pepper

### Preparation
Rinse and drain the kidney beans. Peel the onion and slice it finely. Wipe and slice the mushrooms. Chop the arugula roughly. Make the dressing by mixing all the ingredients together.

Arrange the arugula on a serving dish. Mix the dressing with the mushrooms, onion and beans, and arrange them on top of the arugula to serve.

## 107 Melon and mozzarella skewers

Serves 4

### Ingredients
- ½ cantaloupe melon
- 4 scallions
- 1 pound mini mozzarella balls

### Preparation
De-seed the melon, and use a melon baller to cut as many melon balls as you can. Trim the scallions and cut them into short lengths. Drain the mozzarella balls. Using toothpicks, assemble mini skewers with melon balls, mozzarella balls, and pieces of scallion.

## 108 Caponata Siciliana

Serves 4

### Ingredients
- 1 pound eggplant
- 1 onion
- 1 celery heart
- 1 tablespoon capers
- ¼ cup olive oil
- ⅔ cup canned diced tomatoes
- ¼ cup pine nuts
- ⅔ cup pitted black olives
- Salt and freshly ground black pepper
- 2 teaspoons brown sugar
- 2 tablespoons red wine vinegar

### Preparation

Trim and chop the eggplant into small cubes. Peel and chop the onion. Chop the celery finely, put in a colander and pour over a kettle of boiling water to blanch it. Rinse the capers in water.

Heat half of the oil in a 3-quart pan and sauté the eggplant until brown, about five minutes. Remove the eggplant from the pan and set aside. Pour the remaining oil into the pan and gently sauté the onion until soft. Stir in the blanched celery, diced tomatoes, pine nuts, olives, and capers and sauté gently until the celery is cooked, about five minutes. Season with salt and pepper.

Mix the eggplant into the sauce, add the sugar and vinegar and cook gently for a further 10 minutes. Serve warm or cold with crackers or breadsticks.

## 109 Hot pepper salsa

Serves 4

### Ingredients
- 1 yellow bell pepper
- 4 tomatoes
- 1 or 2 hot yellow or red chili peppers
- ½ onion
- 2 cloves garlic
- Juice 1 lime
- 2 tablespoons white wine vinegar
- ½ teaspoon salt

### Preparation

De-seed and finely chop the bell pepper, tomatoes, and chili peppers. Peel and finely chop the onion. Peel and crush the garlic. Put all the ingredients into a pan and cook gently for 15 minutes. Let cool before serving.

*Yellow and orange tomatoes look wonderful in this dish, if they are available. The heat of the salsa depends on your choice of chili peppers!*

## 110 Chilled tomato soup

Serves 4

### Ingredients
- 2 pounds ripe tomatoes
- 1 onion
- 1 clove garlic
- ¼ cup salted butter
- 1 teaspoon brown sugar
- Pinch of cayenne pepper
- Salt and freshly ground black pepper

### Preparation

Roughly chop the tomatoes. Peel and chop the onion and the garlic. Melt the butter in a 3-quart pan and gently sauté the onions until they are soft. Stir in the garlic and cook for a few minutes more, then add the tomatoes. Cook over a medium heat, stirring frequently, until the tomatoes are beginning to disintegrate. Mix in 1¼ cups water, the sugar and the cayenne pepper and simmer for 10 more minutes. Cool, then transfer to a food processor and blend until very smooth. Season to taste, then chill thoroughly before serving.

*Tomato soup does not have to be hot, especially at this time of year. The most famous chilled soup is Spanish tomato gazpacho, but this one is a little different.*

## 111 Spinach salad with beets and navy beans

Serves 4

### Ingredients
- 1 pound baby spinach
- 1 red onion
- 4 small pickled beets
- 1 x 15-ounce can navy beans

### For the dressing
- 2 cloves garlic
- 5 tablespoons olive oil
- 2 tablespoons red wine vinegar
- 1 teaspoon Dijon mustard
- Salt and freshly ground black pepper

### Preparation

Shred the spinach. Peel and very finely slice the onion. Slice the beets thinly. Drain and rinse the navy beans.

To make the dressing, peel and crush the garlic and combine with all the remaining ingredients. Beat together.

Arrange the spinach on a serving dish, top with the beet and beans and pour the dressing over the top. Serve immediately.

## 112 Apple, pineapple, and cheese salad

Serves 4

### Ingredients
- 3 apples
- Juice 1 lemon
- ½ red onion
- 1 pound fresh pineapple
- 7 ounces Cheddar cheese
- ¼ cup sour cream
- 2 tablespoons mayonnaise

### Preparation
Core and slice the apples and put in a bowl with the lemon juice to prevent them from browning. Peel and finely chop the onion. Cut the pineapple into bite-size pieces. Shred the cheese. Mix the sour cream and mayonnaise together. Combine all the salad ingredients thoroughly and chill before serving.

*Any other flavorful vegetarian hard cheeses work well here too.*

## 113 Golden beet salad

Serves 4

### Ingredients
- 1 golden beet
- 3 broccoli stems
- 2 carrots
- ⅔ cup cashew nuts
- ⅔ cup golden raisins

### For the dressing
- 1 shallot
- 1 clove garlic
- Juice ½ lemon
- 2 tablespoons maple syrup
- 2 tablespoons Dijon mustard
- ½ cup olive oil

### Preparation
Peel the beet, broccoli stems, and carrots and cut into matchsticks. Put the cashew nuts into a heavy pan and dry-roast for around four minutes, stirring frequently until they begin to color. Turn them onto a plate to stop them from cooking further.

To make the dressing, peel and chop the shallot and garlic and put them in a food processor with the other dressing ingredients. Whiz to combine. Toss all the ingredients together in a serving bowl and serve immediately.

# Five ways with zucchini

## 114

### Battered

Slice zucchini, dip them in a light beer batter and fry for a very special summer treat. To make the batter, beat together 1 cup all-purpose flour, ¼ cup cornstarch, ⅔ cup light beer and ⅔ cup soda water. Dust the battered slices with hot paprika and serve with a sour cream and chive dip.

## 115

### Crispy kofta

Mix shredded zucchini with chickpea (gram) flour and garam masala to make a stiff paste, then fry small balls until crisp and golden. Serve as finger food with a mango chutney dip.

## 116

### Stuffed trio

Your favorite pepper stuffing can also be used in zucchini. Halve lengthwise and scoop out the seeds, stuff, and bake under foil in a medium-heat oven for 25 minutes, until tender. Try serving a pretty trio of stuffed zucchini, tomato, and pepper.

## 117

### Grilled slices

Thinly slice zucchini lengthwise, brush with olive oil and put in a hot grill pan. Avoid moving them until you turn them—this way you'll get clear stripes on the flesh.

## 118

### Raw glory

Raw-food enthusiasts use fine strips of zucchini like pasta, serving it with a spicy raw tomato sauce. Use a potato peeler or invest in a spiralizer to get really long, thin zucchini ribbons.

## 119 Mushrooms stuffed with bulgur wheat

Serves 4

### Ingredients

- 6 large Portobello mushrooms
- 1 small onion
- ½ green bell pepper
- 1 tablespoon olive oil
- 1 teaspoon wholegrain mustard
- ⅓ cup cracked bulgur wheat
- Salt and freshly ground black pepper

### Preparation

Preheat the oven to 375°F.

Wipe the mushrooms and remove and discard the stalks. Peel and finely chop the onion. Finely chop the green bell pepper.

Heat the oil and gently sauté the onion and green bell pepper for two minutes, then stir in the mustard, bulgur wheat, chopped mushroom stalks, and ⅔ cup of water. Bring to a boil, then turn down the heat and simmer, covered, for 10 minutes or until the bulgur wheat has absorbed all the water. Season generously with salt and pepper.

Put the mushrooms upside down in a lightly greased baking dish and divide the filling between them. Drizzle with a little extra olive oil and cook for 15 minutes, until heated through.

## 120 Puy lentil salad with snow peas and broccoli

Serves 4

### Ingredients

- 1 cup Puy lentils
- 1 quart vegetable bouillon
- 5 ounces broccoli
- 5 ounces snow peas
- ⅓ cup edamame beans

### For the dressing

- 1 clove garlic
- 2 tablespoons canola oil
- Juice 1 lemon
- 2 tablespoons soy sauce
- ½ teaspoon dried red pepper flakes
- 1 tablespoon honey

### Preparation

Cook the lentils in the bouillon for 15 minutes, until tender but not disintegrating. Drain and set aside to cool. Cut the broccoli into small florets. Bring a 3-quart pan of water to a boil and blanch the broccoli, snow peas, and edamame beans for two minutes. Drain and refresh under cold water.

To make the dressing, peel and crush the garlic, and combine with all the remaining ingredients. Mix well. Toss the cooked vegetables, lentils, and dressing together and serve chilled.

## 121 Fruit and nut coleslaw

Serves 4

### Ingredients
- 4 ounces cabbage
- 2 carrots
- 1 red apple
- $\frac{1}{2}$ cup dried apricots
- 3 tablespoons mayonnaise
- 3 tablespoons crème fraîche or
  sour cream
- Salt and freshly ground black pepper
- $\frac{1}{3}$ cup raisins
- 3 tablespoons pecan pieces

### Preparation
Finely shred the cabbage. Peel the
carrots, if necessary, and coarsely shred.
Finely chop the apple and the apricots.
Mix the mayonnaise and crème fraîche
together and season well.

Put all the ingredients into a large
serving bowl, add the raisins and
pecan pieces, and mix thoroughly.
Serve immediately.

## 122 Watermelon and feta salad

Serves 4

### Ingredients
- 2 pounds watermelon,
  preferably seedless
- $\frac{1}{2}$ red onion
- $\frac{1}{2}$ pound feta cheese
- Handful fresh mint
- Juice $\frac{1}{2}$ lemon
- $\frac{1}{4}$ cup olive oil

### Preparation
Cut away the rind of the melon and cut
the flesh into bite-size pieces, removing
any seeds. Peel and finely slice the
onion. Cut the feta cheese into small
cubes. Chop the mint. Mix the lemon
juice and olive oil together.

Put the watermelon onto a large
serving plate, top with the onion, feta,
and mint, then pour the dressing over
the salad just before serving.

# 123 Garden salad

Serves 4

## Ingredients
- ½ pound baby potatoes
- 5 ounces French or romano beans
- Few fresh chives
- Few sprigs fresh parsley
- 2 tablespoons plain yogurt
- 2 tablespoons mayonnaise
- 1 tablespoon wholegrain mustard
- Salt and freshly ground blackpepper
- 2 ounces baby romaine lettuce
- 2 ounces radishes
- 4 scallions
- 10 cherry tomatoes

## Preparation
Cook the potatoes in boiling, salted water until tender, about 10 minutes depending on their size. Trim and chop the beans into short lengths. Add these to the potatoes for the last five minutes of cooking. Drain the beans and potatoes, and refresh them under cold running water, then set aside to drain and cool.

Chop the chives and the parsley. Mix the yogurt, mayonnaise, mustard, and chopped herbs together thoroughly. Season with salt and pepper to taste.

Shred the lettuce and slice the radishes finely. Trim and chop the scallions. Cut the tomatoes into halves or quarters. Mix all the ingredients together in a large bowl and serve immediately.

# 124 Stuffed tomatoes

Serves 4

### Ingredients

- 1 onion
- 3 cloves garlic
- ½ cup pitted black olives
- 8 large ripe tomatoes
- 1 tablespoon olive oil
- Few sprigs fresh parsley
- ⅓ cup basmati rice
- ¼ cup dry white wine
- ½ cup vegetable bouillon
- Salt and freshly ground black pepper

### Preparation

Preheat the oven to 350°F.

Peel and chop the onion, and peel and crush the garlic. Roughly chop the olives. Slice the tops off the tomatoes and set the tops aside for later. Scoop out the flesh and reserve this too. Chop the fresh parsley. Heat the oil in a 3-quart pan and gently sauté the onion and garlic until soft. Stir in the reserved tomato flesh, olives, and parsley. Heat through, then stir in the rice, wine, and bouillon. Bring to a boil, reduce to a simmer and cook, covered, for 15 minutes. Season to taste.

Spoon the filling carefully into the tomatoes and put them in a greased, shallow baking dish. Replace the tomato tops and bake for 30 minutes, until the rice is tender and the tomatoes are soft.

*Long-grain basmati rice absorbs the moisture in the stuffing without losing its shape or texture. Tomatoes, olives, parsley, and garlic are natural partners and this is an attractive way to deliver some traditional rustic flavors.*

## 125 Roasted beets with basil

Serves 4

### Ingredients
- 6 beets
- 6 cloves garlic
- Handful of fresh basil
- Salt and freshly ground black pepper
- 2 tablespoons olive oil

### Preparation
Preheat the oven to 350°F.

Peel the beets and cut them into quarters. Leave the skin on the garlic, but cut each clove in half lengthwise. Leave the basil intact, no need to chop it up.

Toss all the ingredients together and wrap in a well-sealed parcel of aluminum foil or a roasting bag. Bake for 40 minutes, until the beets are tender.

## 126 Herb polenta cakes

Makes 12

### Ingredients
- 2 cups vegetable bouillon
- ¾ cup polenta
- 4 ounces vegetarian ricotta cheese
- 2 tablespoons chopped fresh herbs: any combination of tarragon, basil, thyme, and parsley
- ¼ stick salted butter

### Preparation
Put the bouillon into a 3-quart pan and bring to a boil. Gradually beat in the polenta and cook, stirring continuously, for two minutes. Remove from the heat and stir in the cheese and herbs. Transfer to a shallow, greased baking dish and chill for 30 minutes until firm.

When the polenta is firm and cold, turn it out of the dish and use a small round cutter (approximately 3 inches in diameter) to press out the polenta cakes. Gently sauté the cakes in the butter for around five minutes, until crisp and golden on both sides.

*These are perfect with simply prepared summer vegetables or asparagus spears.*

## 127 Roasted summer vegetables

Serves 4

### Ingredients

- 3 zucchini
- 1 small eggplant
- 3 red, orange, or yellow bell peppers
- 1 red onion
- 4 cloves garlic
- 3 tablespoons olive oil
- 2 teaspoons fennel seeds

### Preparation

Preheat the oven to 425°F.

Trim and slice the zucchini, eggplant, and peppers. Peel and slice the onion. Leave the garlic skin intact. Put the vegetables into a large mixing bowl and toss with the olive oil and fennel seeds. Spread out on a baking sheet and cook for 30 minutes, stirring occasionally, until the vegetables are soft and browning.

Serve hot, advising your diners to squeeze the soft roast garlic flesh out of the crisp skins, carefully mixing it with the rest of the vegetables.

*If you want to serve this dish cold, retrieve the garlic and squeeze the soft garlic flesh into a dressing of balsamic vinegar and olive oil. Toss through the dish just before serving.*

## 128 Classic pizza base

Serves 4

### Ingredients

- 3 cups bread flour
- 1 teaspoon salt
- 1 tablespoon sugar
- 1 package (¼ ounce) active dry yeast
- 2 tablespoons olive oil

### Preparation

Preheat the oven to 450°F.

Mix the flour, salt, sugar, and yeast together in a large bowl. Stir in the oil and 1 cup warm water. Turn the mixture onto a floured worktop and knead for five minutes, until smooth and elastic. Divide the dough into four equal pieces and roll each piece into a 6-inch circle. Put on a lightly oiled baking sheet and leave in a warm place to rise for 15 minutes. Cover the bases with the toppings of your choice and bake for 10 minutes.

*Try topping with Roasted Summer Vegetables (see left), classic tomato sauce and mozzarella, or try something more adventurous such as mushrooms and goat cheese, overleaf.*

## 129 Mushroom and tomato pizza

Serves 4

### Ingredients
- 1 onion
- 3 ounces mixed mushrooms
- 1 large ripe tomato
- Few sprigs fresh thyme
- 1 tablespoon olive oil
- Salt and freshly ground black pepper
- 3 ounces crumbly goat cheese

### Preparation

Peel and chop the onion finely. Wipe, trim, and slice the mushrooms. Peel, de-seed, and slice the tomato. Strip the thyme leaves from their stalks and finely chop. Heat the olive oil in a skillet and gently sauté the onion and mushrooms together until the onions are soft. Stir in the chopped thyme, salt, and pepper.

Prepare four small pizza bases (see page 101). Divide the mushroom mixture between the bases and top with the tomato slices and crumbled goat cheese. Bake according to the pizza base recipe.

*A mixture of interesting mushrooms gives new interest and texture to this international favorite. Don't overcook the mushrooms; remember they'll be finished in the oven.*

## 130 Zucchini and paprika fritters

Serves 4

### Ingredients
- 3 zucchini
- ¾ cup all-purpose flour
- 1 teaspoon paprika
- 1 teaspoon ground cumin
- Pinch salt
- Vegetable oil, for the pan

### Preparation

Trim and slice the zucchini. Mix together the flour, spices, and salt and spread over a plate.

Heat the oil in a large skillet. Dip the zucchini into the spiced flour, coating both sides, and then fry gently for up to four minutes, until golden and crisp.

## 131 Stuffed red bell peppers

Serves 4

### Ingredients
- 3 ounces whole-wheat couscous
- Handful fresh cilantro
- Juice 1 lemon
- 4 ounces cherry tomatoes
- Salt and freshly ground black pepper
- 4 red bell peppers

### Preparation

Preheat the oven to 350°F.

Spread the couscous out in a large shallow dish and just cover with boiling water. Allow to sit for 15 minutes until the water is absorbed, then fluff gently with a fork. Chop the cilantro and mix into the couscous with the lemon juice. Cut the tomatoes into quarters and mix into the couscous. Season to taste with salt and pepper.

Cut the peppers in half lengthwise and remove the seeds. Carefully fill each half with the couscous mixture, and put on a greased baking sheet. Cook for 20 minutes, until the peppers are soft and the couscous is heated through.

## 132 Fritto misto
Serves 4

### Ingredients
- 2 pounds mixed summer vegetables:
  baby carrots, baby zucchini, sugar
  snap peas, snow peas, bell peppers,
  scallions, onions
- 1 lemon
- 1 cup plus 2 tablespoons
  all-purpose flour
- 1 tablespoon olive oil
- 2 large egg whites
- Canola oil, for the pan

### Preparation
Trim the vegetables, peel if necessary,
and chop into bite-size pieces. Cut the
lemon into wedges.

Put the flour into a large mixing
bowl and make a well in the center.
Gradually mix in the olive oil along
with sufficient warm water to make
a smooth, thin batter. Beat the egg
whites to stiff peaks and fold them into
the mixture.

Fill a 12 x 3-inch skillet or wok to a
depth of 1 inch with canola oil. Dip
the vegetables into the batter and
shallow fry in small batches until crisp
and golden. Serve immediately with
lemon wedges.

*This is a lovely summery appetizer or light
main dish using the season's freshest
baby vegetables. Don't overwhelm them
with the batter—a little is enough.*

## 133 Brazil nut burgers
Serves 4

### Ingredients
- $2/3$ cup Brazil nuts
- 1 onion
- 1 carrot
- 1 large egg
- 1 tablespoon canola oil
- 1 ¾ cups fresh bread crumbs
- 2 tablespoons sun-dried
  tomato paste
- 1 teaspoon dried thyme
- Salt and freshly ground black pepper

### Preparation
Put the nuts into a food processor and
process to a powder. Peel and finely
chop the onion. Peel and shred the
carrots. Beat the egg.

Heat the oil in a skillet and gently
sauté the onion until it is soft. Transfer
to a mixing bowl and mix in the nuts,
bread crumbs, egg, carrots, tomato
paste, and thyme. Season to taste with
salt and pepper.

Divide the mixture into four equal
portions and shape each into a burger.
Put on a parchment paper-lined baking
sheet and brush with a little more oil.
Broil, turning gently, until browned on
both sides.

# Five ways with tomatoes

## 134

### Speedy gratin

For a quick and inexpensive lunch, cover ripe tomatoes and a sprig of rosemary with bread crumbs, garlic, and diced cheese. Drizzle with olive oil and bake at 375°F for 30 minutes.

## 135

### Sun-dried quarters

Make your own sun-dried tomatoes by quartering cherry tomatoes and tossing them in olive oil. Space them out on a parchment paper-lined baking sheet and bake for four hours at 225°F—or the lowest temperature your oven offers.

## 136

### Baked on the vine

Simply put a whole stalk of tomatoes on a baking sheet and roast at 400°F for 10 minutes, until the tomatoes begin to color and split. Serve with a simple plate of scrambled eggs on toast and a good twist of fresh black pepper.

## 137

### Italian Caprese salad

Arrange slices of ripe tomato and buffalo mozzarella on a plate. Garnish with torn basil and dress with a splash of balsamic vinegar and olive oil.

## 138

### Shallow-fried

Get the best out of the end-of-season green tomatoes by serving them up Southern style. Slice them, dredge them in seasoned cornmeal and shallow fry on both sides until browned and crisp.

## 139 Tofu mushroom burgers

Serves 4

V

### Ingredients
- ½ pound firm tofu
- 4 cups fresh bread crumbs
- 1 onion
- 2 carrots
- 4 ounces button mushrooms
- 2 cloves garlic
- Few sprigs fresh tarragon
- 2 tablespoons canola oil, plus extra for the pan
- 1 teaspoon sun-dried tomato paste
- 1 tablespoon soy sauce
- 1 tablespoon peanut butter

### Preparation
Press and drain the tofu and mash it together with the bread crumbs in a large mixing bowl. Peel and finely chop the onion. Peel and shred the carrots. Wipe and slice the mushrooms. Peel and crush the garlic. Chop the tarragon.

Heat the oil in a 12-inch skillet and gently sauté the onion, mushrooms, carrots, and garlic until the onions are soft and translucent. Add the cooked vegetables to the tofu mixture, along with the tomato paste, soy sauce, peanut butter, and tarragon. Mix together thoroughly. Shape into eight small burgers and shallow fry until brown and crisp on both sides.

*Be sure to buy firm tofu for these burgers. The best way to mix the ingredients together is to use your hands — if you want to involve children with cooking, this is the perfect job for them!*

# 140 Summer vegetable ketchup
Serves 4

### Ingredients
- 2 onions
- 2 ribs celery
- 3 carrots
- 3 cloves garlic
- Sprig fresh sage
- Sprig fresh rosemary
- ¼ cup olive oil
- 1 bay leaf
- 3½ pounds ripe tomatoes
- ⅓ cup brown sugar
- ½ cup red wine vinegar
- 1 teaspoon salt
- 1 teaspoon cayenne pepper

### Preparation
Peel and finely chop the onion. Trim and finely chop the celery and the carrots. Peel and crush the garlic. Strip the sage and rosemary from their stalks and finely chop.

Heat the olive oil in a 3-quart pan and gently sauté the onion, celery, and carrots until soft. Add the garlic and bay leaf, and cook for a further minute or two. Remove the bay leaf and put the mixture into a food processor. Blend until smooth.

Pour boiling water into a bowl and skin the tomatoes by plunging them first into the hot water and then into a bowl of cold water. The skins should split and slide off easily. Put half of the skinned tomatoes into the food processor and process until smooth. Return to the pan with the rest of the tomatoes and the other ingredients. Bring to a boil and then simmer, covered, for 30 minutes. Pour into sterilized jars, seal and use within three months.

## 141 Green bell pepper soufflé omelet

Serves 4

### Ingredients

- ½ onion
- 1 green bell pepper
- 2 large eggs
- 4 ounces vegetarian ricotta cheese
- Freshly ground black pepper
- 2 teaspoons canola oil

### Preparation

Peel and finely chop the onion. De-seed and finely chop the bell pepper. Separate the eggs. Beat the egg yolks with the ricotta and 1 tablespoon water until smooth and season to taste with black pepper. Beat the egg whites to stiff peaks and gently fold into the ricotta with the onion and pepper.

Heat the oil in an 8-inch, non-stick skillet and cook the mixture gently for up to six minutes, until golden brown on the bottom. Put the skillet under a preheated broiler to brown the top. Use a spatula to loosen the omelet from the pan and serve immediately.

*Ricotta cheese is not always suitable for vegetarians — check the label to see if it has been made with animal rennet.*

## 142 Potato and scallion frittata

Serves 4

### Ingredients

- 12 ounces baby potatoes
- 6 scallions
- Handful fresh basil
- 4 large eggs
- 2 tablespoons olive oil
- Salt and freshly ground black pepper

### Preparation

Cook the potatoes in a pan of boiling salted water until tender and cooked through, about 10 minutes. Drain, and when cool enough to handle, thickly slice. Trim and chop the scallions. Chop the basil. Beat the eggs.

Heat the oil in an 8 x 2-inch non-stick skillet and sauté the sliced potatoes for up to 10 minutes, until browned and crisp. Mix the eggs together with the scallions, basil, and seasoning. Pour the eggs into the skillet on top of the potatoes and stir quickly to mix through. Cook the frittata on a low heat until it is almost completely set.

Preheat the broiler, then put the skillet under the broiler for three minutes to finish the cooking. Eat hot or cold.

*If your skillet doesn't have a metal handle, don't put it under the broiler. Instead, turn the frittata by taking the pan off the heat, covering it with a plate and carefully turning the pan and plate over. It's best to wear an oven glove, as there may be some hot oil spillage! Then slide the frittata from the plate back into the pan and continue to cook on the other side for a further three minutes.*

# 143 Zucchini and tomato galette

Serves 4

## Ingredients

- 3 zucchini
- 8 ripe tomatoes
- 4 cloves garlic
- ¼ cup canola oil
- 1 teaspoon paprika
- 1 tablespoon sun-dried tomato paste
- 1 large egg
- 3 cups cooked brown rice
- 1 tablespoon soy sauce
- Salt and freshly ground black pepper
- Oil, for greasing and drizzling

## Preparation

Preheat the oven to 400°F.

Grease and line an 11-inch springform cake pan with parchment paper.

Trim and thinly slice the zucchini. Roughly chop the tomatoes. Peel and crush the garlic. Heat the oil in a 4-quart pan or wok and stir-fry the zucchini for up to five minutes, until beginning to brown. Add the garlic, tomatoes, paprika, and tomato paste. Cook on a high heat for two minutes, then reduce the heat and simmer, covered, for 10 minutes. Season to taste with salt and pepper.

Beat the egg. Mix the cooked rice with 2 tablespoons of the zucchini mixture, the egg, and the soy sauce. Put half the rice mixture into the prepared pan, press down firmly with the back of the spoon and smooth the top. Cover with the zucchini and tomato mixture.

Carefully spoon the rest of the rice on top, and gently smooth it over the top of the galette.

Drizzle over a little more oil and bake for 25 minutes, until golden and crisp. Allow to rest for five minutes before releasing the pan and slicing. Serve hot or cold.

## 144 Cheese gougères
Serves 4

**Ingredients**
- 4 ounces Cheddar cheese
- 1 stick salted butter
- ½ teaspoon salt
- 1 cup plus 2 tablespoons all-purpose flour
- 4 large eggs

**Preparation**
Preheat the oven to 425°F.

Shred the cheese. Put the butter and salt into a pan with 1 cup of water. Bring to a boil, then reduce the heat to low and add the flour in a single batch. Stir rapidly and continuously with a wooden spoon as the mixture comes together. Cook for up to three minutes, until the mixture forms a smooth ball. Take the pan off the heat and let it cool for a few minutes.

Beat the eggs. Add them to the warm dough one at a time, beating thoroughly to incorporate. Finally, mix in the shredded cheese. Put small spoonfuls of the mixture onto a parchment paper-lined baking sheet, leaving room between each spoonful for the pastry to puff up. Bake for 10 minutes, turn the heat down to 350°F and cook for a further 15 minutes, until the pastries are cooked through and golden.

Serve warm or cold as canapés, or make a meal by placing five or six balls in a shallow bowl with a simple tomato sauce.

*Choux pastry, or pâte à choux, is a French favorite—classically, it is used to make sweet profiteroles but it can be used in savory dishes too. These gougères should be crisp and golden on the outside, and light and fluffy within.*

# Sweet-and-sour summer vegetables

Serves 4

**V**

### Ingredients

- 6 ounces baby potatoes
- 3 ounces each of carrots, zucchini, and mushrooms
- ½ medium red bell pepper
- ¼ large apple
- ¼ cup water chestnuts
- 1 ½ cups vegetable bouillon
- ⅓ cup canned diced tomatoes

### For the sauce

- 4 ounces onions
- 1 clove garlic
- 1 tablespoon canola oil
- 1 tablespoon tomato purée
- 1 tablespoon soy sauce
- 2 tablespoons white wine vinegar
- 1 teaspoon ground ginger
- 2 teaspoons soft brown sugar
- Salt and freshly ground black pepper
- 2 teaspoons arrowroot

### Preparation

Peel the potatoes and chop into small pieces. Peel the carrots and slice finely. Trim and slice the zucchini. Slice the mushrooms. De-seed and slice the bell pepper. Core and slice the apple. Slice the water chestnuts.

Put the potatoes, carrots, bell pepper, and apple into a 3-quart pan. Add the bouillon—reserving ¼ cup. Cook until tender, drain and set aside. Put 2 tablespoons of the reserved bouillon into a 12-inch skillet and cook the remaining vegetables for five minutes, until tender.

To make the sauce, peel and finely chop the onions and peel and crush the garlic. Warm the oil in a 3-quart pan and sauté the onions until soft. Stir in the garlic. Add the rest of the ingredients, except for the arrowroot. Mix this with the last of the bouillon and add to the sauce. Add the vegetables and bring to a boil. Reduce the heat and simmer for five minutes until the sauce is glossy.

## 146 Grilled corn with garlic sauce

Serves 4

### Ingredients
- 4 ears of corn, husks still on

### For the sauce
- 4 cloves garlic
- 1 cup fresh white bread crumbs
- ½ cup ground almonds
- Juice 1 lemon
- ⅔ cup olive oil
- Salt and freshly ground black pepper

### Preparation
Carefully fold back the leaves of each ear of corn, pull out the silks and fold the leaves back into place. Put the corn into a bowl, cover with water, and soak for 15 minutes. Drain, shake off any excess water, and put the whole ears of corn onto a grill. Cook for around 40 minutes, turning occasionally, until the kernels are soft and juicy, and come away from the cob easily.

Peel and crush the garlic. Put the bread crumbs into a small bowl, cover with water and leave to soak for five minutes. Drain the water, squeeze the bread crumbs to remove as much water as you can, and then put into a blender with the ground almonds, garlic, and lemon juice. Blend to a smooth paste, then gradually pour in the olive oil, keeping the motor running, until the sauce is the consistency of mayonnaise. Season to taste. When the corn is ready, pull back the leaves and smear the garlic sauce over the exposed kernels before eating.

## 147 Basque-style piperade

Serves 4

### Ingredients

- 4 bell peppers (a mixture of colors)
- 2 red onions
- 2 cloves garlic
- 5 tomatoes
- 2 tablespoons olive oil
- Salt and freshly ground black pepper
- 4 large eggs
- ¼ cup 2% milk

### Preparation

De-seed and slice the peppers. Peel and slice the onions. Peel and crush the garlic. Peel and slice the tomatoes.

Heat the oil in a large, heavy pan and gently sauté the onions, peppers, and garlic for a minute. Turn the heat to a minimum, cover the pan and allow the vegetables to "sweat" for five minutes, stirring occasionally, until the peppers are soft. Season with salt and pepper.

Beat the eggs and milk together, then stir into the hot vegetables, keeping the pan on a medium heat. Stir continuously until the egg is cooked and well mixed with the vegetables. Serve immediately.

*This hearty rustic dish has its roots in the Basque country between France and Spain. Try it for breakfast as well as lunch and dinner!*

## 148 Apple cider-baked baby potatoes

Serves 4

### Ingredients

- 1 pound baby potatoes
- 4 shallots
- 2 tart apples
- 4 ounces Lancashire, Colby or American cheese
- ⅔ cup apple cider, juice or hard cider

### Preparation

Preheat the oven to 375°F.

Scrub the potatoes if necessary and slice them approximately ¼ inch thick. Peel and finely slice the shallots. Core and thinly slice the apples. Shred the cheese.

Layer the potatoes, shallots, apples, and cheese into a lightly greased baking dish, ending with a layer of cheese. Pour the cider over the dish, cover with aluminum foil and bake for one hour, until the potatoes and apples are cooked through and tender.

## 149 Baked baby potatoes in parchment parcels

*V*

Serves 4

### Ingredients
- 2 pounds baby potatoes
- 4 tablespoons olive oil
- 4 sprigs of herbs: any combination of sage, rosemary and thyme
- 4 cloves garlic
- Salt and freshly ground black pepper

### Preparation
Preheat the oven to 400°F.

Clean the potatoes but leave the skins on. Put them into a large bowl and toss with the oil, whole herb sprigs, unpeeled garlic cloves, and salt and pepper.

Put the mixed ingredients on a large sheet of parchment paper and fold up the edges to make a parcel. Transfer to a baking sheet and cook for 45 minutes, until the potatoes are tender.

## 150 Grilled sweet potato with aioli

Serves 4

### Ingredients
- 1 pound sweet potatoes
- 4 tablespoons olive oil

### For the aioli
- 5 cloves garlic
- 2 egg yolks
- Juice 1 lemon
- 1½ cups olive oil
- Salt and freshly ground black pepper

### Preparation
Preheat grill. Peel the sweet potatoes and cut into slices about ¼ inch thick. Brush with olive oil and grill for about five minutes on each side until tender.

To make the aioli, peel and crush the garlic. Put it into a blender with the egg yolks and half of the lemon juice. Blend briefly to mix the ingredients together, then, with the motor running, gradually pour in the olive oil to make a thick mayonnaise. Season to taste with salt and pepper, and more lemon juice if you like. Serve the sweet potato slices hot with the aioli on the side.

# 151 Marinated vegetable kebabs

Serves 4

### Ingredients

- 1 red bell pepper
- 1 yellow bell pepper
- 2 zucchini
- 1 red onion
- 6 button mushrooms

### For the marinade

- 1 ½ cups vegetable oil
- Juice 1 lemon
- 2 bay leaves
- 4 tablespoons fresh chopped herbs:
  any combination of parsley,
  thyme, basil, mint, oregano
- 2 cloves garlic
- 1 teaspoon ground cumin
- ½ teaspoon cayenne pepper

### Preparation

Preheat broiler or grill. Cut the peppers into pieces approximately 1-inch square. Slice the zucchini into pieces approximately 1-inch thick. Peel the onion and cut into eighths. Cut the mushrooms in half.

To make the marinade, mix together the oil, lemon juice, bay leaves, fresh herbs, garlic, and spices. Put the prepared vegetables into a large shallow dish and cover with the marinade. Cover with a lid and let soak for at least one hour, stirring occasionally.

Divide the marinated vegetables between eight large skewers and broil or grill, turning frequently, for up to 15 minutes, until cooked through and browned in places.

*Think about how you will thread the cut vegetables onto the skewer as you prepare them—they should all be roughly the same size so that they cook evenly. Pieces that are too thin may burn or fall off the skewer!*

# 152 Mediterranean vegetable loaf

Serves 4

**V**

## Ingredients

- 3 red bell peppers
- 3 yellow bell peppers
- 5 tablespoons olive oil
- 1 eggplant
- 2 zucchini
- 1 red onion
- Handful basil
- Handful black olives
- 1¾ pounds crusty white bread loaf
- 2 tablespoons vegetarian or vegan pesto

## Preparation

Preheat the oven to 425°F.

De-seed and slice the bell peppers, put on a baking sheet, toss with 2 tablespoons olive oil and cook for up to 20 minutes, until soft. Transfer the peppers to a sealable plastic food bag, close, and let cool. Peel the skins off the bell peppers and discard. Trim and slice the eggplant and zucchini, and toss with the remaining oil. Grill in small batches, leaving undisturbed on the hot pan to get clear stripes. Set aside to cool. Peel and finely chop the onion. Chop the herbs and olives.

Slice the bread in half, lengthwise, and scoop out the soft bread inside to make two crusty shells. Layer the cooked vegetables into the bread shells, dotting each layer with onion, pesto, olives, and basil. Sandwich the filled bread halves back together, press together firmly and wrap tightly in plastic wrap. Refrigerate for an hour, then slice carefully to serve.

# 153 Crunchy stuffed zucchini

Serves 4

## Ingredients

- 1 onion
- 3 tomatoes
- 1 red bell pepper
- 1 cup cooked chickpeas
- 4 large zucchini
- 1 tablespoon olive oil
- 2 teaspoons dried thyme
- 4 ounces Cheddar cheese
- 4 ounces plain yogurt
- ½ teaspoon paprika
- 1 ounce plain potato chips

## Preparation

Preheat the oven to 400°F.

Peel and finely chop the onion. Skin and chop the tomatoes. De-seed and chop the red bell pepper. Drain and rinse the chickpeas. Halve the zucchini lengthwise and, using a teaspoon, scoop out the flesh, leaving shells about ¼ inch thick. Reserve the flesh.

Heat the olive oil and gently sauté the onion, zucchini flesh, pepper, tomatoes, chickpeas, and thyme for five minutes, until softened.

Put the zucchini shells into a lightly greased baking dish and divide the filling between the shells. Shred the cheese and mix it with the yogurt and paprika. Spoon the cheese mixture over the filled zucchini. Crush the potato chips and sprinkle them over the dish. Bake for 20 minutes, until heated through and crispy on top.

## 154 Zucchini and herb penne
Serves 4

### Ingredients
- 4 zucchini
- 1 clove garlic
- ¼ cup olive oil
- 1 bay leaf
- 1 whole, dried red chili pepper
- Small handful fresh basil
- Small handful fresh parsley
- 5 scallions
- 1 pound penne
- Salt and freshly ground black pepper

### Preparation
Trim and slice the zucchini. Peel the garlic, but leave it whole. Warm the olive oil in a 12-inch skillet or wok and gently cook the garlic, bay leaf, and chili pepper until the garlic is golden. Scoop the garlic, bay leaf, and chili pepper out of the oil and discard them. Sauté the zucchini in the same oil for about four minutes, until soft but not disintegrating. Roughly chop the basil and parsley, and trim and finely chop the scallions.

Cook the pasta in boiling salted water, until tender, about nine to 10 minutes, and drain. Add the pasta to the zucchini in the skillet. Stir in the basil, parsley, and scallions and cook gently for three minutes, until the dish is heated through. Season to taste with salt and pepper.

*Other pasta can be used, but tube-shaped penne holds its shape well and makes a nice textural and visual contrast with the softened vegetables.*

## 155 Twice-cooked summer vegetables

Serves 4

### Ingredients
- 1 onion
- 2 cloves garlic
- 2 red bell peppers
- 2 yellow bell peppers
- 4 ounces French or romano beans
- 1 large potato
- ¼ cup olive oil
- Salt and freshly ground black pepper

### Preparation

Peel and slice the onion. Peel and crush the garlic. De-seed and slice the bell peppers. Trim and slice the French beans into thin strips. Peel the potato and cut into fine matchsticks.

Toss the prepared vegetables together with the olive oil and put into a 4-quart flameproof casserole dish. Stir-fry for two minutes, then reduce the heat to minimum, cover and sweat for 15 minutes, until the potatoes are tender. Season to taste with salt and pepper, and serve hot.

*Stir-frying the vegetables before sweating them gently means that they will be soft and succulent.*

## 156 Leek and lemon linguine

Serves 4

### Ingredients
- 4 leeks
- 2 cloves garlic
- Handful fresh basil
- Handful fresh arugula
- 3 tablespoons olive oil
- ¼ cup dry white wine
- 1 lemon
- 1 ½ cup crème fraîche or sour cream
- 2 ounces vegetarian Parmesan-style cheese
- 10 ounces linguine
- Salt and freshly ground black pepper

### Preparation

Trim and finely slice the leeks. Peel and crush the garlic. Chop the fresh herbs. Zest and juice the lemon. Warm the oil in a 3-quart pan and gently fry the leeks until soft. Stir in the garlic and cook for a further minute, then add the wine, lemon juice, and lemon zest. Cook on a low heat for five minutes. Stir in the crème fraîche and vegetarian Parmesan-style cheese.

Cook the pasta in salted boiling water, until tender. Drain and add to the leeks with the chopped basil and arugula. Stir together and heat through to serve. Season to taste with salt and pepper.

# 157 Lentils spiced with harissa

Serves 4

### Ingredients
- 1⅓ cups brown lentils
- 1 onion
- 3 cloves garlic
- 1 teaspoon cumin seeds
- 1 cinnamon stick
- 2 tablespoons olive oil
- 1 teaspoon harissa paste
- 1 teaspoon chili powder, or to taste
- 2 bay leaves
- Salt and freshly ground black pepper

### Preparation
Rinse the lentils and put them into a 3-quart heavy pan. Cover with 2½ cups of water, bring to a boil and simmer, covered, for 20 minutes until the lentils are soft but not mushy. Drain the lentils, reserving the cooking water for later.

Peel and finely chop the onion. Peel and crush the garlic. Crush the cumin seeds with the back of a spoon, cracking them just to let the flavor out.

Heat the oil in a 3-quart heavy pan and gently sauté the onion until soft and translucent. Stir in the garlic, the harissa, and all the spices. Stir-fry for two minutes, then add the lentils, the bay leaves and 1 cup of the reserved cooking liquid. Simmer, uncovered, on a very low heat for 20 minutes and serve warm.

*Harissa is a spicy paste made from puréed red bell peppers and chili peppers. Although it originated in Tunisia, it is widely used in Arabic countries. Ingredients vary, but it may include garlic, cumin, coriander, lemon juice, and caraway seeds.*

## 158 Summer ratatouille
Serves 4

### Ingredients
- ½ pound onions
- 2 cloves garlic
- ½ pound zucchini
- 2 red bell peppers
- ½ pound summer squash
- 1 x 15-ounce can chickpeas
- Few sprigs fresh parsley
- 1 vegetable bouillon cube
- 2 tablespoons olive oil
- 2 x 15-ounce cans diced tomatoes
- Salt and freshly ground black pepper

### Preparation
Peel and roughly chop the onions. Peel and chop the garlic.
Trim and slice the zucchini. De-seed and slice the peppers.
Peel the squash and chop it into bite-size pieces. Drain and
rinse the chickpeas. Finely chop the parsley. Crumble the
bouillon cube to a powder.

In a flameproof casserole dish, sauté the onion in the olive oil
until soft, then add the garlic and cook for another minute.
Add all the other ingredients, cover and simmer on a very low
heat for 30 minutes.

*This is a traditional stewed vegetable dish from the Provence
region of France, which has found its way onto the menu in many
other countries. Eggplant and zucchini are key ingredients but
other vegetables can be incorporated  into the mix depending on
what is abundant at the time.*

# 159 Zucchini and tomato tart.

Serves 4

### Ingredients

- 1 sheet pie crust, thawed, if frozen
- 4 zucchini
- 1 pound ripe cherry tomatoes
- 4 ounces Gruyère cheese
- 3 tablespoons vegetarian Parmesan-style cheese
- Handful fresh basil
- 4 large eggs
- 1 cup crème fraîche
- $\frac{1}{3}$ cup 2% milk
- 1 tablespoon olive oil

### Preparation

Preheat the oven to 400°F.

Use the pie crust to line an 8-inch pie pan, Refrigerate for 20 minutes, then line with baking parchment, fill with baking beans and bake for 15 minutes. Remove the beans and paper and return to the oven for a further five minutes. Take the pie crust out of the oven and set aside. Turn the oven temperature down to 350°F.

Trim and thinly slice the zucchini. Halve the cherry tomatoes. Shred the Gruyère cheese and vegetarian Parmesan-style cheese. Chop the basil. Beat the eggs together with the milk and the crème fraîche. Gently sauté the zucchini slices in the olive oil until beginning to brown, about five minutes.

Put a layer of zucchini (about half of them) into the pie crust shell and cover with a layer of cherry tomatoes and a layer of Gruyère cheese. Add the rest of the zucchini, the basil, and the tomatoes. Mix the remaining Gruyère cheese into the egg mixture and carefully pour this over the top of the vegetables. Sprinkle with vegetarian Parmesan-style cheese and bake for 40 minutes, until set and golden.

*Gruyère cheese adds an intriguing flavor to this tart. It has a strong taste, which means you don't have to use a lot to get a great cheesy taste, and it's not as greasy as some other hard cheeses*

## 160 Sparkling peach sangria

Serves 4

### Ingredients
- ¼ cup brown sugar
- 3 large, ripe peaches
- 2 cups dry white wine
- ⅓ cup Grand Marnier
- Sparkling white wine, to serve

### Preparation
Put the sugar into a 1½-quart pan with ¾ cup of water and heat gently, stirring, until the sugar dissolves. Take off the heat and let cool.

Peel and pit the peaches, and slice them roughly. Put into the bowl of a food processor with the cooled sugar syrup and process until very smooth. Mix with the dry white wine and Grand Marnier, cover and chill for an hour. Pass the liquid through a muslin-lined sieve, squeezing out as much of the juice as possible. Dilute to taste with sparkling wine.

## 161 Strawberry smoothie

Serves 4

### Ingredients
- 7 ounces fresh strawberries
- 1 cup plain yogurt
- ½ cup chilled 2% milk
- Vanilla extract, to taste
- Honey, to taste

### Preparation
Blend the strawberries, yogurt, and milk until smooth. Adjust the flavor to suit your taste with vanilla extract and honey.

## 162 Pink lemonade
Serves 4

**V**

### Ingredients
- 2 lemons
- 1 ¼ cups sugar
- 1 pound fresh raspberries
- Sparkling mineral water, ice
- Fresh mint sprigs, to garnish

### Preparation
Slice the lemons and put them into a 3-quart pan with the sugar and raspberries.

Add 1 ½ cups of water and bring to a boil. Make sure the sugar is dissolved, then remove from the heat and let cool. Press through a sieve to make a cordial that can be stored, refrigerated, for one week.

To serve, mix with sparkling water and ice, then top with a sprig of fresh mint.

## 163 Iced green tea
Serves 4

### Ingredients
- Small handful fresh mint
- 3 green tea bags
- 2 tablespoons honey

### Preparation
Finely chop the mint. Steep all the ingredients in 1 quart boiling water for five minutes, then remove the teabags and chill thoroughly before serving.

*Make an alcoholic version by adding Japanese sake according to your own taste.*

## 164 Egg-free carrot cake

Serves 4

### Ingredients
- ½ pound carrots
- 2 cups self-rising flour
- 1 tablespoon cinnamon
- 1 teaspoon nutmeg
- 1 stick unsalted butter
- ⅓ cup honey
- ½ cup sugar

### Preparation

Preheat the oven to 325°F. Grease a 10-inch round springform cake pan.

Peel and shred the carrots. Sift the flour and spices together in a large mixing bowl. Melt the butter in a 1½-quart pan, add the honey and sugar and stir over a gentle heat until the sugar is dissolved. Pour the sugar and butter mixture into the spiced flour, add the carrots and mix well.

Spoon the mixture into the prepared pan and bake for around 75 minutes, until a skewer inserted into the center of the cake comes out clean. Let the cake cool in the pan for 10 minutes before turning out. Decorate with confectioners' sugar and tiny carrot decorations if available.

*The secret to success is the long, slow bake for this cake—keep the oven temperature low and be patient! Vegans can substitute maple syrup for the honey and vegan margarine for butter in this recipe. Carrot decorations can often be found in the home baking section of supermarkets, or in specialty kitchenware shops.*

## 165 Vegan lemon-and-lime cheesecake

Serves 6

### Ingredients

- 1 lemon
- 1 lime
- 12 ounces graham crackers
- 6 ounces vegan margarine
- ¼ cup agave nectar
- ¼ cup cornstarch
- 14 ounces silken tofu

### Preparation

Zest and juice the lemon and the lime. Crush the crackers into fine crumbs. Melt the margarine in a 1 ½-quart pan and mix with the cracker crumbs. Press the mixture into the base of a 8-inch springform pan, using the back of a spoon to smooth it into a firm crust. Let cool.

In a 1 ½-quart pan, mix the agave nectar with a scant 2 cups of water and blend in the cornstarch. Gradually heat to boiling point, beating continuously to prevent any lumps from forming. Once boiling point is reached, reduce the heat and continue to stir until the mixture thickens.

Combine the thickened syrup mixture with the silken tofu and fruit zest and juice and beat until smooth. Spoon over the prepared base, smooth the top and chill for two hours before serving.

## 166 Melon and ginger cream

Serves 4

### Ingredients

- 1 Charentais melon
- 4 pieces preserved stem ginger
- ⅔ cup heavy cream
- 1 cup Greek yogurt
- 4 ginger snaps

### Preparation

Cut the melon in half and scoop out the seeds. Cut away the skin and chop the flesh into small pieces. Chop the ginger very finely. Beat the cream lightly and then mix it with the yogurt, melon, and half of the ginger. Spoon into four serving dishes and top with the remaining ginger. Chill for 30 minutes, and then serve each portion with a ginger snap.

## 167 Strawberry crush

Serves 4

### Ingredients
- 14 ounces quark or light cream cheese
- 1 tablespoon sugar
- Juice 1 lemon
- 14 ounces hulled strawberries
- Sprig fresh mint

### Preparation
Put the quark, sugar, and lemon juice into a large bowl and mix well. Put the strawberries into another bowl and crush them with the back of a fork, so that they are broken up but not completely mashed. Stir the fruit and quark together and spoon into four serving dishes. Chill and garnish with fresh mint to serve.

## 168 Cherry almond granola

Serves 4

### Ingredients
- 3¾ cups rolled oats
- 2 tablespoons pumpkin seeds
- 2 tablespoons sunflower seeds
- 2 tablespoons sesame seeds
- 1½ cups slivered almonds
- 1 teaspoon almond extract
- ½ cup maple syrup
- 2 tablespoons canola oil
- ⅔ cup dried cherries

### Preparation
Preheat the oven to 300°F.

Mix all the ingredients together except the dried cherries. Spread the mixture over a parchment-lined baking sheet and bake for 15 minutes. Stir up the mixture adding in the dried cherries and return to the oven for up to 15 more minutes, until golden. Turn onto a cold baking sheet to cool—it will crisp up more. Store in an airtight container for up to one month.

# 169 Yogurt and strawberry tart
Serves 8

**Ingredients**
- ¾ stick unsalted butter
- 1 ½ cups all-purpose flour
- 1 tablespoon confectioners' sugar
- 1 large egg yolk
- Sprig fresh mint

**For the filling**
- 3 ½ cups low-fat plain yogurt
- 1 cup sugar
- 1 teaspoon vanilla extract
- 6 ounces fresh hulled strawberries

**Preparation**

The night before, line a large sieve with several sheets of paper towels and place it over a large bowl. Put the yogurt into the sieve and leave it overnight in the refrigerator to drain.

To make the pastry, cut the butter into small pieces and blend into the flour with your fingertips. Stir in the confectioners' sugar and the egg yolk. Mix well, then gradually add cold water, a splash at a time, until the dough comes together and is soft but not sticky. Gather the pastry into a ball, wrap in a plastic bag and chill for about 20 minutes.

Preheat the oven to 375°F. Roll out the pastry thinly and line an 8- to 9-inch tart dish. Prick the base and set aside for 20 minutes, then line the base with parchment paper and fill with baking beans. Bake for 15 minutes, remove the beans and paper and return to the oven for five more minutes. Set aside to cool.

Mix the thickened yogurt with the sugar and vanilla extract. Arrange the strawberries in the pastry shell, spoon the yogurt mixture on top and smooth it out. Chill for two hours before serving, and garnish with a little finely chopped fresh mint.

*This smooth and refreshing tart is perfect for a warm outdoor dinner party or an afternoon tea. Straining the yogurt is important because it will make the filling firmer and dryer.*

## 170 Crème pâtissière

Serves 4

### Ingredients

- 1 large egg plus 1 egg yolk
- ¼ cup sugar
- 2 tablespoons all-purpose flour
- 1½ cups 2% milk
- Few drops vanilla extract

### Preparation

Beat the egg and egg yolk with the sugar, then gradually beat in the flour and milk. Transfer the mixture to a 1½-quart saucepan and bring to a boil, whisking continuously. Simmer for about three minutes, then remove from the heat and stir in the vanilla extract. Pour the mixture into a shallow dish to cool, and stir occasionally to prevent a skin from forming.

*Crème pâtissière is a useful addition to any cook's repertoire. This recipe can be used as a filling for fruit tarts, eclairs, or cakes.*

## 171 Summer fruit tart

Serves 6

### Ingredients

- ⅓ cup apricot preserves
- 1 sweet pastry shell (see page 146)
- 1 recipe crème pâtissière (see left)
- 1½ pounds mixed summer fruits: strawberries, raspberries, blueberries, kiwi fruit, mandarin orange segments

### Preparation

Put the preserves into a small saucepan with 1 tablespoon water and heat gently, stirring, to make a syrup. Use a pastry brush to brush the base of the pastry shell with the syrup and let cool—this will help to keep the base of the tart crisp. Fill the tart with crème pâtissière and cover with a decorative arrangement of your chosen fruit. Brush with the remaining preserve syrup and serve at room temperature.

## 172 Blackberry fool

Serves 4

**Ingredients**
- 1¾ cup blackberries
- 2 tablespoons honey
- 2 tablespoons crème fraîche or sour cream
- ½ cup plain yogurt

**Preparation**

Put the blackberries into a food processor and blend until liquidized. Pass the mixture through a sieve and discard the seeds. Sweeten the blackberry pulp with the honey. Mix the crème fraîche into the yogurt. Gently swirl the blackberry mixture into the yogurt. Serve chilled.

## 173 Green tea and orange compote

Serves 4

**Ingredients**
- 3 green tea bags
- Zest 1 unwaxed orange
- 2 tablespoons honey
- 1 pound mixed dried fruit: apricots, golden raisins, raisins, figs, pears, and apples

**Preparation**

Cut any large pieces of fruit into bite-size pieces. Steep the teabags in 2½ cups boiling water for five minutes, then squeeze the teabags and discard them. Put the tea into a 3-quart pan and add the orange zest and honey. Warm gently to dissolve the honey and mix well, then stir in the mixed fruit and simmer for 15 minutes. Let cool and store, refrigerated, for up to one week.

## 174 White chocolate and hazelnut soufflé

Serves 4

### Ingredients
- 4 large eggs
- 1 cup all-purpose flour
- ¾ cup 2% milk
- ¾ cup sugar
- 4 ounces white chocolate
- ⅓ cup toasted hazelnuts

### For the soufflé molds
- ¼ stick unsalted butter
- 2 tablespoons sugar

### Preparation
Preheat the oven to 325°F.

Separate the eggs into yolks and whites. In a small saucepan, mix the yolks with the flour, milk, and sugar and heat gently, stirring constantly, until the mixture thickens. Melt the white chocolate in a small heatproof bowl over a pan of hot water and then mix into the flour mixture. Let cool. Put the toasted hazelnuts into a food processor and process to a powder.

Melt the butter and brush liberally onto the insides of four individual soufflé molds. Spoon a little sugar into each mold and tip it so that the sugar sticks to the butter, covering the surface. Tap out any excess.

Fold the ground nuts into the chocolate mixture. Beat the egg whites to stiff peaks and fold them very gently into the chocolate mixture. Spoon the mixture into the molds and bake for 18 minutes until well risen and just firm. Serve immediately, as they will start to sink as soon as you take them out of the oven.

*Since the French invented soufflés, it seems that the whole world has been experimenting with sweet and savory variations! These elegant individual soufflés have a delicious nutty flavor.*

## 175 Coconut cake
Serves 8

### Ingredients
- 7 ounces creamed coconut
- 3 tablespoons canola oil
- 7 ounces cream cheese
- 2 cups sugar
- 3 tablespoons rose water
- 1 teaspoon vanilla extract
- 6 large eggs
- 3⅓ cups all-purpose flour
- 2 tablespoons ground almonds
- 2½ cups unsweetened shredded coconut

### Preparation
Preheat the oven to 325°F. Grease and line an 8 x 3-inch round cake pan.

Shred the creamed coconut and melt it gently in a pan or in the microwave. Stir in the canola oil and set aside to cool. Beat the cream cheese and sugar together, then mix in the creamed coconut and canola oil mixture, rose water, vanilla extract, and eggs. Beat the mixture until fluffy, and then fold in the flour, ground almonds, and shredded coconut.

Spoon into the prepared pan and bake for approximately one hour until a skewer inserted into the center of the cake comes out clean. Turn out onto a cooling rack and let cool before slicing.

*Creamed coconut is made from the finely shredded, dehydrated flesh of coconuts. It is usually sold in blocks, and is different from coconut cream, which is like coconut milk but much thicker and richer.*

## 176 Vegan coconut panna cotta
Serves 4

### Ingredients
- 1½ cups coconut milk
- 4 tablespoons sugar
- 1 tablespoon agar agar flakes
- ½ cup plain or vanilla soy yogurt
- 1 teaspoon vanilla extract (omit if using vanilla yogurt)

### Preparation
Pour the coconut milk and sugar into a 1½-quart saucepan and beat in the agar agar flakes. Let stand for five minutes, then heat and simmer for five minutes, stirring constantly. Remove the mixture from the heat and push it through a fine sieve. Mix in the yogurt and vanilla extract and pour into four ramekins. Chill for at least two hours before turning out to serve.

# Five ways with strawberries

## 177

### Floral accents

Make a simple dish of fresh strawberries into a special event by serving it with a home-made sugar syrup flavored with lavender flowers, geranium leaves, mint, elderflowers, or orange zest.

## 178

### Summer pudding

This dessert has a long history, and that's because it's perfect for using up a glut of fresh fruit and some bread. Line a large bowl with sliced bread and fill with ripe strawberries. Cover with bread and chill. Turn out onto a vintage plate.

## 179

### Dairy delight

Gently crush ripe strawberries, swirl into some whipped cream, Greek yogurt or crème fraîche and chill to serve.

## 180

### Flavor enhancers

The sweet, tart flavor of strawberries are complemented by black pepper and balsamic vinegar. It sounds wrong, but try drizzling a little balsamic syrup over a bowl of strawberries, or surprise guests by offering a twist of black pepper at the table.

## 181

### Quick strawberry sauce

Cook strawberries with a splash of orange juice, and sugar to taste, until they are soft but not disintegrating. Serve cold with yogurt or ice cream.

## 182 Strawberry and elderflower tart

Serves 6

### Ingredients

- ¾ stick unsalted butter
- 1½ cups all-purpose flour
- 1 tablespoon confectioners' sugar
- 1 large egg yolk

### For the filling

- 1¼ pounds strawberries
- 2 tablespoons elderflower cordial
- ¾ cup sugar
- 2 tablespoons cornstarch

### Preparation

To make the sweet pastry shell, cut the butter into small pieces and blend into the flour with your fingertips. Stir in the confectioners' sugar and the egg yolk. Mix well, then gradually add cold water, a splash at a time, until the dough comes together and is soft but not sticky. Gather into a ball, wrap in a plastic food bag and chill for 20 minutes.

Preheat the oven to 375°F. Roll the pastry out thinly and line a 8- to 9-inch fluted pie pan. Prick the shell and set aside to rest for a further 20 minutes. Line the shell with parchment paper and fill with baking beans. Bake for 15 minutes, remove the beans and paper and return to the oven for five more minutes. Set aside.

Put 7 ounces of the strawberries into a food processor and process until smooth. Pour into a saucepan and mix in the cordial and sugar. Mix the cornstarch with a little water and then stir into the fruit with ⅔ cup more water. Bring to a boil, stirring as the mixture thickens. Remove from the heat and let cool.

Mix the remaining strawberries into the mixture and then pour into the pastry shell. Chill well before serving.

*Strawberries and elderflowers together are the very essence of summer! Stirring fresh strawberries into the glossy sauce adds texture and an extra layer of flavor to this dish.*

# 183 New York cheesecake

Serves 4

### Ingredients
- 1 stick unsalted butter
- 6 ounces graham crackers
- 1½ pound cream cheese
- Generous ¾ cup sugar
- 2 teaspoons vanilla extract
- 4 large eggs

### For the topping
- 2 cups sour cream
- 2 tablespoons sugar
- ½ teaspoon vanilla extract

### Preparation
Preheat the oven to 350°F.

Melt the butter in a 1½-quart saucepan. Finely crush the graham crackers. Mix the cracker crumbs with the melted butter and press the mixture into the bottom of a 10-inch springform pan, using the back of a spoon to smooth it out and pressing the base into place firmly.

Mix the cream cheese with the sugar and vanilla extract. Beat the eggs and gradually add them to the cream cheese, without over-beating the mixture. Spoon into the pan, smooth the top and bake for 30 minutes.

To make the topping, mix the sour cream, sugar and vanilla extract together. After the cheesecake has baked for 30 minutes, take it out of the oven, pour the topping over the top and return it to the oven to bake for a further 10 minutes. Let cool and chill completely before removing from the pan and serving.

# 184 Valencia orange tart

Serves 6–8

## Ingredients

- 1 cup all-purpose flour
- 2 tablespoons unsweetened cocoa powder
- ½ cup sugar
- ¼ teaspoon salt
- 1 stick cold, unsalted butter, cut into small cubes
- 1 large egg

## For the filling

- 4 medium oranges
- ½ cup cornstarch
- 1 cup sugar
- 6 large egg yolks

## For the topping

- 2 ½ cups fresh orange juice
- ¾ cup sugar, plus more for caramelizing the tart
- 1 tablespoon shredded orange zest
- 4 to 5 thin-skinned oranges, scrubbed well
- Orange marmalade

## Preparation

Preheat the oven to 350°F. Blend the dry ingredients in a food processor, add the butter and pulse to create small pebbles. Mix the egg yolk with a little water and add to the machine while running. Pulse in short bursts until the mixture is crumbly, then turn onto plastic wrap and gather together. Chill for 30 minutes.

Roll the dough out and press it into an 11-inch tart pan with removable base. Chill in the pan for at least 30 minutes. Prick the bottom of the crust with a fork and bake for 12 minutes, rotating halfway through. Remove and let cool.

To make the filling, zest and juice the oranges and put into a bowl. Stir in the cornstarch until smooth. Bring 2 cups of water to boil in a 3-quart pan and add the cornflour mixture. Whisk until thick and glossy, and remove from the heat. Put the egg yolks and sugar into a medium-sized bowl and beat them together until well combined. Stir the egg mixture into the filling, return the pan to the heat and whisk until the eggs are cooked and the mixture becomes very thick. Allow to cool, then spoon into the pastry shell.

To make the topping, mix the juice, sugar, and zest in a wide pan and bring to a simmer over medium-high heat, stirring frequently. Slice the oranges about ⅛-inch thick and add to the juice. Simmer, partially covered, for about 15 minutes. Let the oranges cool, then drain, discard the liquid, and pat the slices dry with paper towels.

Turn up the oven to 375°F. Spread the marmalade on top of the filling and lay on the orange slices, overlapping them slightly. Bake for 30 minutes, until the oranges are very soft and lightly browned.

# Fall

# Fresh in Season ...

### Pumpkins and squashes

Winter squashes should be firm—a few blemishes on the skin don't really matter unless you're serving the whole vegetable, stuffed and baked. Small squashes can be baked whole, hollowed out and used as bowls for salads or soups.

### Mushrooms

Lots of different mixed mushrooms are available in spring and summer, but they are most plentiful and varied during the fall. Washing them makes them soggy, so just use paper towels or a soft brush to gently take off any specks of dirt.

### Onions

Generally, the larger the onion, the milder the taste. Red onions are sweeter than brown onions and are the best choice for using raw in salads. Shallots have a delicate flavor—covering them with boiling water makes them easier to peel.

### Sunchokes

Knobbly little roots with a sweet nutty flavor, these are relatives of the sunflower and no relation to globe artichokes, despite their other name of Jerusalem artichokes. Scrub them with a vegetable brush and steam them, then slice and serve warm with butter or an oil-based dressing.

### Okra

Also called lady's fingers, okra is an unripe seed pod and should be eaten while it is young and green as older specimens can be fibrous. It adds a thick, almost gluey consistency to stews, which some love and others hate!

### Savoy cabbage

This cabbage has distinctive wrinkled leaves that are dark green on the outside and paler inside. Slice the leaves crosswise into ribbons and stir-fry with onion and garlic, or blanch whole leaves and fold them around a savory stuffing mixture.

### Leeks

Soil and grit can become trapped inside leeks as they grow. To avoid a nasty crunch, cut off the root and any tough green leaves, then halve the leek lengthways, put into a sink full of cold water and separate the layers to clean them.

### Endive

Endive heads should have greenish-white crisp leaves, firmly packed together. Sliced, they add a refreshing bitter taste to salads and whole leaves can serve as tiny edible plates for canapés.

## 185 Sun-dried tomato and pumpkin seed pâté

Serves 4

### Ingredients
- 1 cup pumpkin seeds
- 8 sun-dried tomato halves in oil
- 1 clove garlic
- 2 tablespoons lemon juice
- 1 tablespoon soy sauce
- 1 large date
- ½ red chili pepper
- 2 scallions

### Preparation

The night before, soak the pumpkin seeds in cold water for six hours. Rinse and drain.

Whiz all of the ingredients except the scallions in a food processor until semi-smooth. Decant the mixture into a small bowl. Finely chop the scallions and mix into the bowl, reserving a few pieces to garnish.

Serve in individual ramekins with thickly sliced fresh bread or toast.

## 186 Thai-style mushrooms in endive leaves

Makes about 30 canapés

### Ingredients
- 5 ounces shiitake mushrooms
- 2½ ounces radishes
- ½ small red bell pepper
- 6 heads of endive

### For the marinade
- 1 teaspoon chopped green chili pepper
- ½ inch ginger root
- ½ teaspoon garlic
- 2 tablespoons soy sauce
- 1 lime
- 1 tablespoon honey

### Preparation

Start with the marinade. Finely chop the ginger root, and zest and juice the lime. Mix all the marinade ingredients in a bowl.

Chop the mushrooms, radishes, and bell pepper and marinate. Stir thoroughly. Cover and refrigerate for one hour.

Cut off the bases of the endive and take them apart. Set aside the hearts for use in a salad. Put a heaped teaspoon of the mushroom mixture into each of the larger leaves.

# 187 Leek and potato soup

Serves 4

## Ingredients

- 1 tablespoon cumin seeds
- 1 pound leeks
- ½ pound potatoes
- ½ stick salted butter
- 2½ cups vegetable bouillon
- 1¼ cups 2% milk
- ⅓ cup half and half
- Salt and freshly ground
  white pepper
- Chili oil (optional)

## Preparation

Dry-roast the cumin seeds in a heavy pan for a minute or two, until they begin to release their aroma. Remove from the heat and set aside.

Peel and slice the leeks and potatoes. In a 4-quart pan, melt the butter and cook the leeks and potatoes, covered, for around 10 minutes, until soft but not colored. Add the vegetable bouillon, bring to a boil and simmer, covered, for around 20 minutes, until the potatoes are tender.

Let cool slightly before blending in a blender or food processor. Stir in the milk and half and half, and adjust the seasoning to taste. Reheat to serve, topped with a few toasted cumin seeds and a drop of chili oil.

# 188 Extra quick cornbread

Makes 9

## Ingredients

- ⅔ cup all-purpose flour
- ⅔ cup cornmeal
- 1½ teaspoons baking powder
- ½ teaspoon salt
- 1 large egg
- ⅔ cup 2% milk
- 1 tablespoon honey
- 1 tablespoon olive oil
- 1 green chili pepper (optional)

## Preparation

Preheat the oven to 400°F. Grease a 7-inch round baking pan or a 9-hole muffin pan.

Sift the flour, cornmeal, baking powder, and salt together in a large bowl. In a separate bowl, beat the egg and add the milk, honey, and oil. Finely chop the green chili pepper, if using, and add to the bowl of dry ingredients. Mix thoroughly.

Combine the liquid ingredients with the dry ingredients and stir together to make a soft batter. Spoon into the prepared baking pan and bake for around 15 minutes, or until risen, golden brown and firm to the touch.

*Serve warm, in buttered wedges with a bowl of soup or vegetable chili.*

# **189** Carrot and fennel soup

Serves 4

## Ingredients

- 2 fennel bulbs
- 1 rib celery
- 1 onion
- 3 tablespoons olive oil
- 1 pound carrots
- 2 cloves garlic
- 1 quart vegetable bouillon
- 2 tablespoons crème fraîche or sour cream,
  plus extra for serving
- Salt and freshly ground black pepper

## Preparation

Thinly slice the fennel, celery, and onion and sauté in the olive oil until soft but not browned. Peel and chop the carrots and garlic and add to the pan. Cook for another minute or two. Pour in the vegetable bouillon, bring to a boil, cover and simmer for 20 minutes, until carrots are tender.

Remove from the heat, let cool slightly before stirring in the crème fraîche or sour cream. Blend the soup until smooth. Taste and adjust the seasoning, then reheat to serve. Top each bowl with a swirl of cream.

*Fennel has a delicate aniseed flavor that works well with the sweetness of the carrots in this classic soup. Enjoy it hot or cold.*

## 190 Sweet beet salad with orange and coconut

Serves 4

### Ingredients
- 3 beets
- ½ orange
- 2 tablespoons fresh, shredded coconut
- Juice ½ lime
- 2 tablespoons zante currants or small raisins
- 1 teaspoon apple cider vinegar
- 1 teaspoon flaxseed oil

### Preparation
Peel and finely shred the raw beets. Peel and dice the orange. Combine all the ingredients and chill for an hour before serving.

*For an elegant presentation, pack small portions of the salad into ramekins, timbale molds, or espresso cups and turn out onto serving plates.*

## 191 Blackberry and feta salad

Serves 4

### Ingredients
- 4 ounces mixed salad greens
- 4 ounces feta cheese
- 10 ounces blackberries

### For the vinaigrette
- ¼ cup olive oil
- ¼ cup balsamic vinegar
- ¼ cup honey

### Preparation
Arrange the greens on plates and top with crumbled feta and blackberries, keeping about a dozen for the dressing.

To make the dressing, mash the remaining blackberries through a sieve and beat the juice with the olive oil, balsamic vinegar, and honey. Dress each plate individually.

*Remember this recipe when you've found some ripe wild blackberries. The sweet-sharp fruit works perfectly with the salty cheese, and the colors are a treat. Feta also makes a great salad with watermelon (see page 96).*

## 192 Sunchoke salad
Serves 4

### Ingredients
- 1 pound sunchokes
- 1 large endive
- 1 small red bell pepper

### For the dressing
- 2 tablespoons lemon juice
- 2 tablespoons olive oil
- Salt and freshly ground black pepper
- 1 scallion
- Handful fresh dill weed or thyme

### Preparation
Scrub the sunchokes but leave the skins on. Cut them into ¼ inch slices and steam for 12 minutes, until soft but not breaking up. Shred the endive. Slice the red bell pepper into thin matchsticks.

To make the dressing, blend the lemon juice, oil, and seasoning. Finely chop the scallion and herbs and stir in. Toss the vegetables in the dressing.

*This salad is delicious warm or chilled.*

## 193 Walnut and red grape salad
Serves 4

### Ingredients
- 1 tablespoon salted butter
- 2 tablespoons sugar
- ⅓ cup walnuts or pecans
- 2 heads of endive
- 4 ounces arugula
- 2 ounces seedless red grapes
- 4 ounces blue cheese
- Salt and freshly ground black pepper

### For the dressing
- 2 tablespoons olive oil
- 1 tablespoon balsamic vinegar

### Preparation
Heat the butter and sugar in a small pan, add the nuts and cook gently, stirring continuously for five minutes, until crisp. Turn onto a plate to cool slightly.

To make the dressing, blend the oil and vinegar and season to taste.

Cut the bases off the endive, break into leaves and toss with the arugula and dressing. Top the salad with the red grapes, crumbled cheese and caramelized nuts.

# 194 Classic butternut squash soup

Serves 4

### Ingredients
- 2 cloves garlic
- 2 tablespoons olive oil
- 3 sprigs fresh rosemary
- 1 butternut squash
- 2 carrots
- 1 onion
- 1 large potato
- 1 quart vegetable bouillon
- Bouillon, milk, or half and half, to thin
- Salt and freshly ground black pepper

### Preparation
Peel and crush the garlic. Heat the oil in a 4-quart pan and add the garlic and rosemary and warm for one minute. Peel and chop the squash, carrots, and onion, and cube the potato. Add them to the pan and stir. Cook for 10 minutes, stirring regularly, then add the vegetable bouillon, turn down the heat and simmer, covered, for 30 minutes, until the vegetables are meltingly soft.

Allow the soup to cool, remove the rosemary sprigs, and blend until smooth. If the soup is too thick, adjust by adding a little more bouillon, milk, or half and half. Season to taste. Reheat to serve.

*The garlic and rosemary in this soup provide a welcoming aroma that can't be beaten after a walk in the fall woods. Garnish each bowl of soup with a swirl of sour cream, crème fraîche, or herb pesto.*

## 195 Vegan potato salad with apple and celery

Serves 4

### Ingredients
- 4 medium Yukon Gold potatoes
- 3 red-skinned apples
- 1 lemon
- 2 ribs of celery
- ⅓ cup hazelnuts or pecans

### For the vegan mayonnaise
- ⅓ cup chilled soy milk
- 1 clove garlic
- ½ teaspoon mustard
- 2 tablespoons lemon juice
- ⅔ cup vegetable oil

### Preparation
Boil the potatoes leaving the skins on. Let cool and then slice. Core the apples and slice thinly, again leaving the skins on. Cut the lemon in half and squeeze one half over the apples to stop them discoloring. Trim and slice the celery ribs. Roughly crush the nuts with the side of a knife.

To make the mayonnaise, put the chilled soy milk, garlic, and mustard into a blender with rest of the lemon juice. Blend briefly. Then, keeping the motor running, slowly drizzle in the oil and continue blending until the mixture thickens.

Toss all the salad ingredients together with 3 tablespoons of vegan mayonnaise and serve immediately.

## 196 Mushroom pâté with nutmeg and chives

Serves 4

### Ingredients
- 2 shallots
- 2 ounces salted butter
- ½ pound mixed mushrooms
- ½ cup fresh bread crumbs
- 4 ounces cottage cheese
- Pinch nutmeg
- Few fresh chives
- Salt and freshly ground black pepper

### Preparation
Slice the shallots and sauté in the butter until soft but not browned. Wipe and chop the mushrooms and add to the pan. Cover the pan and cook on a very low heat for 15 minutes. Let cool slightly.

Put the mushroom mixture into a food processor with the bread crumbs, cottage cheese, nutmeg, chives, and seasoning. Blend until smooth and transfer into a small bowl. Cover and refrigerate for an hour before serving.

*Serve in individual ramekins with hot toast and a few crisp salad leaves.*

# 197 Walnut and frisée salad

Serves 4

### Ingredients
- ½ pound frisée or curly endive
- ½ pound radicchio
- ¾ cup walnuts

### For the dressing
- Zest and juice ½ orange
- 2 tablespoons walnut oil
- 1 tablespoon olive oil
- 1 tablespoon balsamic vinegar
- 1 tablespoon soy sauce
- 1 teaspoon honey or maple syrup

### Preparation
Trim the salad greens and chop or rip into bite-size pieces. Chop the walnuts roughly and dry-roast in a heavy pan for a few minutes.

To make the dressing, combine all of the ingredients in a bowl. Pour over the salad and mix thoroughly to coat. Sprinkle the nuts on top and serve immediately.

# 198 Spinach and apricot salad

Serves 4

### Ingredients
- ⅔ cup cider vinegar
- 2 tablespoons lemon juice
- ⅔ cup dried apricots
- 1 cup sunflower seeds
- 2 tablespoons soy sauce
- 2 tablespoons olive oil
- Freshly ground black pepper
- 1½ pounds baby leaf spinach

### Preparation
Heat the vinegar to boiling, then remove from heat. Add the lemon juice and put the dried apricots into the hot liquid to soak for 30 minutes.

Dry-roast the sunflower seeds in a heavy pan until they begin to change color. Take the pan off the heat, sprinkle on the soy sauce and mix thoroughly. Quickly scoop the sticky mixture out of the pan and onto a plate to cool.

Drain and chop the apricots, reserving the liquid. Beat the reserved juice with the olive oil and black pepper to taste. Assemble the salad by mixing the spinach with the chopped apricots, sunflower seeds and dressing.

# 199 Creamy mushroom soup

Serves 4

### Ingredients

- 2 onions
- 1 pound mixed mushrooms
- 1 tablespoon olive oil
- 1 teaspoon paprika
- 1 teaspoon caraway seeds
- 2 cups water or vegetable bouillon
- 2 tablespoons margarine
- 3 tablespoons all-purpose flour
- 1 ¼ cups non-dairy milk
- 2 to 3 tablespoons red wine
- Few sprigs fresh parsley

### Preparation

Chop the onions and wipe and slice the mushrooms. In a 4-quart pan, sauté the onion in the olive oil until soft and beginning to brown. Stir in the chopped mushrooms, paprika, and caraway seeds, and cook for five minutes. Pour in the vegetable bouillon or water and simmer, covered, for 15 minutes.

In a separate 1 ½ -quart pan, melt the margarine, add the flour and cook for one minute, stirring constantly. Add the non-dairy milk, a little at a time, beating thoroughly to prevent lumps. Combine the two mixtures, stir well, then simmer, covered, for 15 minutes. Finely chop the parsley. Stir the red wine into the soup just before serving garnished with the parsley.

# 200 Squash salad with grapefruit and almonds

Serves 4

## Ingredients

- ½ cup brown rice
- ½ butternut squash
- 2 tablespoons vegetable oil
- Salt and freshly ground pepper
- ⅔ cup whole, blanched almonds
- Cayenne pepper, to taste
- ½ tablespoon vegetable oil
- Few sprigs fresh mint
- Zest 1 lemon

## For the dressing

- 1 grapefruit
- 1 shallot
- 1 tablespoon honey
- 2 tablespoons olive oil

## Preparation

Preheat the oven to 350°F.

Cook the brown rice in a pan of boiling water for about 20 minutes, until soft. Drain and leave to cool. Peel, de-seed and cut the squash into 1-inch chunks. Toss in vegetable oil, season with salt and pepper and roast in a baking dish for around 30 minutes. Stir and return to the oven for a further 12 minutes, until soft and beginning to brown at the edges. Set aside to cool.

To toast the almonds, increase the oven temperature to 400° F. Put the blanched almonds into a small bowl and combine with the cayenne pepper and vegetable oil. Mix thoroughly and transfer to a baking sheet. Toast for approximately five minutes, until fragrant and browning. The nuts become crisp as they cool. Chop the mint.

To make the citrus dressing, juice the grapefruit and dice the shallot. Combine both with the honey in a blender. Begin processing, and slowly add the olive oil. Adjust seasoning to taste.

To assemble the salad, mix the cooked, cooled butternut squash with the cooked rice and stir in the dressing. Sprinkle the lemon zest on top of the salad with the toasted almond and chopped mint. Serve immediately.

## 201 Warm broccoli salad

Serves 4

### Ingredients

- 1 head broccoli
- 1 clove garlic
- ½ inch ginger root
- 1 teaspoon toasted sesame oil
- ½ teaspoon soy sauce
- ½ teaspoon dried red pepper flakes
- 2 tablespoons cashew pieces

### Preparation

Trim the broccoli and cut the florets into bite-size pieces. Use a vegetable peeler to peel the stalk and chop it into crudité-size sticks. Peel and crush the garlic. Peel and shred the ginger. Warm the sesame oil in a 4-quart pan or wok. Stir-fry the broccoli with the soy sauce, garlic, ginger, red pepper flakes, and cashews for five minutes, until cooked but still crisp. Serve warm.

## 202 Warm roast beet and herb salad

Serves 4

### Ingredients

- 1 ½ pounds beets
- 2 cloves garlic
- Small handful fresh parsley
- Small handful fresh basil
- ¼ cup olive oil
- 1 tablespoon white wine vinegar
- 2 tablespoons capers

### Preparation

Preheat the oven to 325°F.

Roast the whole beets for about an hour. Let cool for 15 minutes until cool enough to handle. Rub off the skin and slice into rounds. Peel and chop the garlic. Chop the parsley and basil. Mix the beets with all the other ingredients and serve warm.

## 203 Apple, walnut, and goat cheese salad

Serves 4

### Ingredients

- ¼ cup walnut pieces
- 2 ribs celery
- 1 green apple
- 1 red apple
- 3 ounces mixed salad greens

### For the dressing

- 4 ounces soft rindless goat cheese
- 2 tablespoons 2% milk
- 1 teaspoon maple syrup
- 1 teaspoon white wine vinegar
- 2 tablespoons olive oil
- Salt and freshly ground black pepper

### Preparation

Make the dressing first. Blend all the ingredients except the salt and pepper together in a food processor or blender. Having the goat cheese at room temperature will help to bring it together smoothly. Taste, and adjust seasoning.

Toast the walnut pieces gently in a dry, heavy pan for up to three minutes, until they begin to brown and release their fragrant oils, then turn onto a plate so that they do not cook any further.

Trim and chop the celery into bite-size pieces. Core and thinly slice the apples, leaving the skins on.

Put the salad on a serving dish, top with the walnuts, apple, and celery and drizzle with dressing, taking care not to swamp the fresh ingredients.

*Celebrate the apple harvest by looking for some unusual or heritage varieties to try in this salad.*

# Five ways with potatoes

## 204
### Rösti

Coarsely shred raw potatoes, mix with finely chopped onion and garlic, and gently pan-fry spoonfuls of the mixture. Cook for five minutes on each side, flattening with the back of an oiled spoon.

## 205
### Spicy wedges

Cut large baking potatoes into wedges, toss with olive oil, smoked paprika and cayenne pepper. Oven roast for 30 minutes at 400°F.

## 206
### Twice baked

Scoop out the center of baked potatoes and mix with chopped onion or finely shredded leek, shredded cheese, and a splash of milk. Pile the stuffing back into the skins and bake in the oven for 15 minutes.

## 207
### Potato salad

Toss boiled baby potatoes in a flavorful vinaigrette or with mayonnaise and chopped scallions. Mix it up by adding a little garlic or fresh chopped herbs, such as chives, sorrel, or dill weed.

## 208
### Sliced and baked

Slice potatoes very thinly using a mandolin or food processor. Layer in a baking dish with finely chopped rosemary, salt, and black pepper. Pour over vegetable bouillon or cream to just cover the potatoes. Cover with foil and bake for an hour at 350°F. Remove the foil for the last 15 minutes of cooking.

# 209 Mushroom tartlets
Serves 4

### Ingredients
- ½ ounce dried mushrooms
- 1 sheet puff pastry
- 14 ounces mixed mushrooms
- 2 tablespoons olive oil
- 2 tablespoons crème fraîche
- 2 egg yolks
- Salt and freshly ground black pepper

### Preparation
Soak the dried mushrooms in boiling water for an hour. Drain and pat dry on paper towels, reserving the water. Using a 2-inch pastry cutter, cut 24 circles from the pastry sheet. Gently press each into a greased mini tart pan. Prick with a fork, then cover and chill.

Preheat the oven to 400°F. Roughly chop the mushrooms and sauté in the olive oil for five minutes. Chop the drained, soaked mushrooms, add to the pan and cook for two minutes more. Let cool, then transfer to a food processor and blend to a rough paste, or chop very finely by hand. Transfer the chopped mushrooms to a large bowl, and beat in the crème fraîche, egg yolks, and seasoning.

Fill each puff-pastry shell with a heaped teaspoon of mixture—they will rise and expand when cooked, so don't overfill. Bake for up to 12 minutes, until golden and springy to the touch. Serve warm with a drizzle of white truffle oil and a sprinkle of finely chopped herbs.

# 210 Mushroom salad
Serves 4

### Ingredients
- 1 pound mixed mushrooms
- 3 ounces mixed salad greens
- ¼ stick salted butter
- Salt and freshly ground black pepper

### For the dressing
- 2 tablespoons olive oil
- Zest ½ lemon
- 1 tablespoon balsamic vinegar

### Preparation
Trim and wipe the mushrooms. This dish looks best if you keep the mushrooms whole—if there are any very large ones, halve or quarter them to match the size of the rest.

Arrange the salad greens on serving plates. Prepare the dressing by mixing the olive oil, lemon zest, and balsamic vinegar together and seasoning to taste.

Melt the butter in a 3-quart heavy pan and gently sauté the mushrooms for three minutes, until heated through but not collapsing. Season with salt and pepper.

Arrange the warm mushrooms, along with any juices, on top of the greens and pour the dressing over the top. Serve warm with thickly sliced fresh bread.

# 211 Roasted onions stuffed with saffron rice

Serves 4

## Ingredients

- 4 large onions
- ½ cup basmati rice
- Pinch saffron strands
- ¼ stick salted butter
- ½ cup pine nuts
- 2 tablespoons golden raisins
- ½ teaspoon ground cardamom
- Salt and freshly ground black pepper
- Olive oil, for greasing
- 1 to 2 teaspoons sugar

## Preparation

Preheat the oven to 400°F.

Put the whole onions, unpeeled, on a baking sheet and roast for 45 minutes. When they are cool enough to handle, carefully trim the bases so that they will stand up, and trim a similar amount off the tops. Then peel the onions and press or scoop out the centers, retaining them for later and leaving the shells of the onions two to three layers thick.

Cook the rice with the saffron in boiling water for 10 minutes, until tender, then drain and set aside.

Finely chop the centers of the onions. Melt the butter in a 12-inch skillet and gently cook the pine nuts for a minute, then stir in the chopped onion, golden raisins, and cardamom and sauté until the onions are soft and translucent. Season to taste with salt and pepper.

Brush the onion shells with olive oil and sprinkle the outsides with a little sugar. Put them on a parchment paper-lined baking sheet and carefully fill them with the stuffing. Return to the oven and bake for 20 minutes, until just browning.

# 212 Red wine mushroom bourguignon

Serves 4

### Ingredients

- 3 large carrots
- 3 ribs celery
- ½ pound button mushrooms
- 4 whole cloves garlic
- 1 pound baby onions
- Few sprigs fresh thyme
- ¼ cup olive oil
- 3 cups vegetable bouillon
- 3 tablespoons tomato paste
- 1 tablespoon vegetarian Worcestershire sauce
- 2½ cups red wine
- 1 tablespoon all-purpose flour
- 2 bay leaves

### Preparation

Trim and chop the carrots and celery. Wipe the mushrooms. Peel the garlic cloves. Peel the baby onions and cut any large ones in half. Strip the thyme leaves from their stalks and finely chop. Heat 2 tablespoons of the olive oil in a 4-quart flameproof casserole dish and sauté the mushrooms for three minutes. Remove with a slotted spoon and set aside. Put the rest of the oil into the pan and sauté the onions, garlic, carrots, and celery until the onions are soft and translucent.

Put the bouillon into a large measuring cup and mix in the tomato paste, Worcestershire sauce, thyme, and wine.

Stir the flour into the vegetables and cook for a minute, then pour in the bouillon mixture and add the bay leaves. Cover and simmer for 20 minutes. Just before serving, stir in the mushrooms and heat through.

*Most brands of Worcestershire sauce contain anchovies and are not suitable for vegetarians. Look for a vegetarian brand in a specialty food shop or in the "healthy" section of the market, or use mushroom ketchup. It's well worth having this versatile and tasty sauce in your store cupboard.*

## 213 Mixed mushroom sauté

Serves 4

### Ingredients

- 4 shallots
- 2 pounds mixed mushrooms
- ½ cup olive oil
- 1 stick salted butter
- 4 cloves garlic
- 3 tablespoons chopped, fresh flat-leaf parsley
- Freshly ground black pepper

### Preparation

Blanch the shallots in a bowl of boiling water for a few minutes to loosen the skins. Peel and finely chop. Wipe the mushrooms, remove and discard any woody stems, then chop into roughly similar sizes—halves, quarters and slices. Gently cook the shallots in the oil for five minutes, until translucent, add the mushrooms and butter, then continue to cook over a medium heat for 10 minutes, stirring often so they don't stick.

Peel, chop, and add the garlic and cook for a further two minutes. Remove from the heat, toss with chopped parsley and black pepper, and serve.

*This works well as a side dish, or as a light meal served with crusty bread or brown rice.*

## 214 Apricot and orange quinoa

Serves 4

### Ingredients

- 10 dried apricots
- Zest and juice ½ orange
- 1¼ cups quinoa
- Small handful fresh, flat-leaf parsley
- 2 tablespoons olive oil
- ⅓ cup pine nuts
- ½ teaspoon cumin
- ⅓ cup toasted slivered almonds

### Preparation

Roughly chop the dried apricots and put them into a small bowl with the orange juice and 3 tablespoons of boiling water. Put the quinoa in a pan, cover with boiling water and simmer for 15 minutes. Turn off the heat and drain away any remaining water, then return the cooked quinoa to the warm pan, cover and allow to rest for five minutes before fluffing with a fork.

Chop the parsley. Drain the soaked apricots and gently mix them into the quinoa along with the orange zest, olive oil, parsley, pine nuts, and cumin. Serve warm, sprinkled with the slivered almonds.

## 215 Warm Japanese hijiki stir-fry

Serves 4

### Ingredients

- 1 ounce dried hijiki seaweed
- 1 tablespoon plus 2 teaspoons soy sauce
- 2 carrots
- 4 ounces baby corn
- 2 scallions
- ½ pound snow peas
- ½ teaspoon dried red pepper flakes
- 1 tablespoon olive oil
- 1 teaspoon roasted sesame oil
- 1 tablespoon water
- 1 teaspoon cider vinegar or rice vinegar
- 1 tablespoon soy sauce
- 1 tablespoon cashew nuts

### Preparation

Soak the hijiki in a pan of cold water for 30 minutes. Add 2 teaspoons of soy sauce to the soaking water, simmer for five minutes, then drain.

Cut the vegetables into pieces: matchstick-size carrots, slices of baby corn, and shredded scallions and snow peas. Put them all into a large bowl with the red pepper flakes, olive oil and roasted sesame oil, and mix thoroughly.

Stir-fry the vegetables in a hot, lightly oiled wok until heated through. Add the hijiki and splash in the water, vinegar, and a tablespoon of soy sauce. Serve topped with a few whole cashews.

*Hijiki is a sea vegetable that is popular in Japan. It is generally sold dried.*

## 216 Warm kale with balsamic figs

Serves 4

### Ingredients

- ½ pound kale

### For the dressing

- 5 dried figs
- 3 tablespoons balsamic vinegar
- ½ cup olive oil
- ¼ teaspoon mild chili powder
- 1 teaspoon lemon juice
- Salt and freshly ground black pepper

### Preparation

Make the dressing first. Put the figs, balsamic vinegar, olive oil, chili powder and lemon juice into a blender and process until smooth and creamy. Adjust seasoning to taste.

To cook the kale, strip out any tough stems, shred the leaves and boil for seven minutes. Drain, toss with the dressing and serve immediately.

## 217 Pumpkin and pear stew with saffron

Serves 4

V

### Ingredients
- 2 cloves garlic
- 4 ounces bread
- 3 tablespoons olive oil
- ½ cup ground almonds
- 1 teaspoon paprika
- 1 onion
- ½ cup dry white wine
- 4 ounces carrots
- 4 ounces pumpkin or squash
- 4 firm pears
- 1 x 15-ounce can diced tomatoes
- Pinch saffron strands
- 1 ¼ cups cooked or canned chickpeas

### Preparation
Preheat the oven to 425°F.

Peel and crush the garlic. Slice the bread thickly and brush with 1 tablespoon of olive oil and crushed garlic. Put on a baking sheet and bake until golden. Let cool, then break into pieces. Blend in a food processor with the almonds and paprika, until smooth.

Chop the onion, and sauté in the remaining olive oil in a 3-quart pan, until soft. Add the wine and 3 cups of water. Bring to a boil.

Peel and slice the carrots. Peel and cube the pumpkin. Core and cube the pear. Add to the saucepan along with the tomatoes and saffron and simmer for 15 minutes until the vegetables are tender. Stir in the bread mixture and the chickpeas, and reheat before serving.

*This hearty stew makes a complete meal, but some crusty bread is perfect for mopping up any last remnants!*

## 218 Steamed lemon vegetable parcels

Serves 4

### Ingredients

- 12 ounces prepared seasonal vegetables: baby carrots, winter squash, broccoli (or broccolini), green beans, scallions, bean sprouts, squash, baby corn, mushrooms and onions
- 1 inch ginger root
- 2 tablespoons olive oil
- Salt and freshly ground black pepper
- 1 lemon
- ¼ cup toasted slivered almonds

### Preparation

Preheat the oven to 400°F.

Choose a mixture of colorful seasonal vegetables and cut them into fine slices. Peel and shred the ginger. Toss the vegetables with the olive oil, ginger and seasoning.

Thinly slice the lemon into rounds and divide between six large squares of parchment paper, then pile the prepared vegetables on top. Sprinkle with toasted slivered almonds and bring the corners of the paper up to form pouches. Secure with natural fiber twine, place on a baking sheet and bake for 15 minutes.

Serve the parcels on individual plates and let guests open them themselves (careful, the steam will hiss!).

## 219 Spinach and ricotta frittata

Makes 12

### Ingredients

- 1 pound spinach
- 9 ounces vegetarian ricotta cheese
- 2 tablespoons crème fraîche
- 2 ounces strong Cheddar cheese
- 4 large eggs
- ¼ cup 2% milk
- ¼ teaspoon hot pepper sauce
- Pinch nutmeg
- Salt and freshly ground black pepper

### Preparation

Preheat the oven to 375°F. Lightly grease a 12-cup muffin pan.

Blanch the spinach for two minutes, until it collapses. Lift out, drain, and squeeze dry. Mix with the ricotta, crème fraîche, and shredded Cheddar cheese. Beat together the eggs, milk, hot pepper sauce, nutmeg, and salt and pepper. Stir into the spinach mixture.

Spoon the mixture into the prepared muffin pan and bake for around 25 minutes, until risen and golden. Let stand for five minutes before removing from the pan.

# 220 Butternut squash and Gruyère tart

Serves 4

## Ingredients

- ½ large butternut squash
- 3 tablespoons olive oil
- Salt and freshly ground black pepper
- ⅓ cup hazelnuts
- 1 large onion
- 2 cloves garlic
- 2 tablespoons dry white wine
- 4 ounces Gruyère cheese
- 1 large egg
- 1 puff pastry sheet

## Preparation

Preheat the oven to 400°F.

Peel and cube the squash and toss with 2 tablespoons of the olive oil, season with salt and pepper, and roast on a greased baking sheet for around 30 minutes, stirring occasionally, until beginning to brown.

Roast the hazelnuts on a baking sheet for five minutes, let cool, and crush coarsely.

Thinly slice the onion and chop the garlic and sauté in a tablespoon of olive oil until brown. Stir in the wine and cook for a further minute. Shred the Gruyère and mix with the roasted squash, adding the onions and hazelnuts. Beat and mix in the egg.

Cut an 8 x 8-inch square from the pastry sheet and put onto a lightly greased baking sheet and, using a sharp knife, score a line approximately ¾ inch inside each edge. Pile the filling onto the pastry and arrange within the scored line—this allows the edges of the tart to puff up during baking. Bake for 15 minutes or until golden and serve immediately.

# 221 Zucchini and rice casserole

Serves 4

## Ingredients

- 3 onions
- 2 cloves garlic
- 1 pound zucchini
- 4 ounces Cheddar cheese
- 2 tablespoons olive oil
- 1 cup vegetable bouillon
- ¾ cup Arborio rice
- 2 large eggs
- ¾ cup plus 2 tablespoons crème fraîche
- ½ teaspoon smoked paprika

## Preparation

Preheat the oven to 425°F.

Peel and finely slice the onions. Peel and crush the garlic. Thinly slice the zucchini. Shred the cheese. Sauté the onions and zucchini in the oil for five minutes, until they begin to soften. Stir in the garlic and cook for a further minute, then add the vegetable bouillon and rice. Bring to a boil and reduce the heat to a minimum. Cover and cook very gently for 20 minutes.

Beat the eggs with the crème fraîche, paprika, and half the cheese. Stir this into the rice mixture, mix well, and transfer to a greased baking dish. Top with the remaining cheese and a little more paprika, and bake for 15 minutes, until the cheese is golden and bubbling.

*Use up the last of the season's zucchini in this satisfying cheesy dish, spiked with delicious smoked paprika.*

## 222 Leeks à la grecque

Serves 4

### Ingredients
- Juice 2 lemons
- ¼ cup olive oil
- ½ cup dry white wine
- 2½ cups water
- 5 celery leaves
- 1 carrot
- 1 small onion
- 10 black peppercorns
- 10 whole coriander seeds
- 1 bay leaf
- 8 leeks
- 1 large egg
- Handful black olives

### Preparation

Mix the lemon juice, oil, wine, and water and put in a 3-quart pan. Peel and chop the celery leaves, carrot, and onion. Add to the saucepan long with the peppercorns, coriander seeds, and bay leaf. Bring to a boil, then simmer, covered, for 10 minutes.

Trim the leeks and cook them in the liquid until tender, about 10 minutes. Hard-cook the egg in the same water, approximately seven minutes. Allow the cooked leeks to cool in the liquid, then remove to a plate. Remove the egg. Reduce the cooking liquid by boiling it fast. Let cool. Chop the egg.

To serve, strain the reduced liquid and pour over the leeks. Garnish with the chopped egg and black olives.

## 223 Broccoli with lemon butter

Serves 4

### Ingredients
- 1 head broccoli
- 3 tablespoons slivered almonds
- ½ stick salted butter
- Zest and juice ½ lemon

### Preparation

Trim the broccoli and cut the florets into bite-size pieces. Use a potato peeler to peel the stalk and slice it thinly into rounds. Steam the broccoli until bright green and tender, about five minutes. Put the slivered almonds into a small, heavy pan and warm them gently until they begin to brown. Remove from the heat and transfer to a plate to prevent burning.

Melt the butter in a small saucepan, then stir in the lemon juice and zest with the toasted almonds. Pour over the warm broccoli and serve immediately.

# Five ways with pumpkin or butternut squash

## 224
### Honey roasted chunks
Toss peeled chunks in a mixture of olive oil and honey and roast at 400°F until tender (about 30 minutes). Stir into a warm salad with some cooked grains, wilted spinach and soft goat cheese.

## 225
### Deep-fried tempura
Peel squash, cut into strips, coat in a beer batter (see page 94) and deep-fry. Serve at once with a dipping sauce of soy sauce, white wine vinegar, honey, sesame oil, and chopped scallions.

## 226
### Fruity kebabs
Skewer peeled chunks of squash or pumpkin, baste with a marinade of pineapple juice, soy sauce, root ginger, garlic, olive oil, and dry sherry, then grill or broil for 10 minutes, turning and basting frequently.

## 227
### Crunchy wedges
Leave the skin on, and cut into ½ inch slices. Add oil, thyme, lemon zest, and crushed garlic and bake at 375°F for 30 minutes.

## 228
### Roasted seeds
Don't waste the seeds! Toss dried seeds with olive oil and season with garlic salt, ground cumin, and coriander or try brown sugar, ground cinnamon, and ginger. Roast at 275°F for 30 minutes. Serve as a snack, or sprinkled onto salad, fruit salad, or oatmeal.

## 229 Tofu in hot sauce
Serves 4

### Ingredients
- 9 ounces firm tofu
- 1 clove garlic
- 1 tablespoon toasted sesame oil
- 1 teaspoon soy sauce
- 1 teaspoon tomato paste
- 1 teaspoon hot paprika
- 1 tablespoon cornstarch
- Fresh cilantro

### Preparation
Drain the tofu and cut into bite-size pieces. Peel and crush the garlic. Warm the oil in a 1-quart pan or wok, and gently fry the garlic for just a moment or two, then remove from the heat.

Put the soy sauce, tomato paste, and paprika into a 1-quart pan with 1 cup cold water. Whisk together well, then beat in the cornstarch. Heat the mixture gradually, stirring constantly, until boiling point is reached. Tip the garlic and oil into the sauce.

Gently stir the tofu into the sauce and heat through to serve. Garnish with sprigs of fresh cilantro.

## 230 Leek and red lentil casserole

Serves 4

### Ingredients

- 1 cup red lentils
- 1 pound leeks
- 1 clove garlic
- 3 large eggs
- 4 ounces strong Cheddar cheese
- 2 tablespoons olive oil
- Sprig fresh rosemary
- ½ cup canned diced tomatoes
- Salt and freshly ground black pepper

### Preparation

Preheat the oven to 400°F.

In a 3-quart pan, cover the lentils with water, bring to a boil and then simmer until completely soft, about 20 minutes. Add more water during cooking as necessary.

Trim and slice the leeks. Crush the garlic, beat the eggs and shred the Cheddar cheese. Sauté the leeks in the olive oil until soft, about five minutes. Add the garlic and rosemary and cook for a minute or two.

Combine the lentils, leeks, and all the remaining ingredients. Mix thoroughly and pile into a greased baking dish. Bake for 30 minutes until set and golden.

## 231 Pan-fried baby carrot barlotto

Serves 4

### Ingredients

- Approximately 2½ cups vegetable bouillon
- 1 cup barley
- 1 tablespoon soy sauce
- 3 tablespoons salted butter
- 2 cloves garlic
- 12 whole baby carrots
- 2 tablespoons vegetable oil
- 4 sprigs fresh thyme
- Salt and freshly ground black pepper

### Preparation

In a 3-quart pan, bring the bouillon to a boil, using just enough to cover the barley. Add a dash of soy sauce and the barley and simmer for 45 minutes. Stir in a tablespoon of butter.

Peel the garlic and halve lengthwise. Sauté the carrots in the oil over a high heat for five minutes, turning frequently. Add the thyme, garlic, and the remaining butter. Stir to coat the carrots, then add ½ cup of bouillon. Season and simmer, covered, for 20 minutes, until the carrots are tender.

Serve the barley topped with the carrots and their cooking liquid.

*A barlotto is a risotto made with barley rather than Arborio rice.*

# 232 Nutty onion tart

Serves 4

### Ingredients
- 2 ounces Cheddar cheese
- 2 ounces unblanched almonds
- 1 ½ cups fresh whole-wheat
  bread crumbs
- Pinch nutmeg
- 2 teaspoons sunflower oil

### For the filling
- 1 large onion
- ½ cup vegetable bouillon
- 1 teaspoon whole-wheat flour
- Few fresh chives
- 1 large egg
- 1 teaspoon Dijon mustard
- ⅔ cup plain yogurt
- Salt and freshly ground black pepper

### Preparation
Preheat the oven to 400°F.

Shred the Cheddar cheese and put into the bowl of a food processor with the almonds and bread crumbs. Process until you have fine crumbs. Stir in the nutmeg and sunflower oil, and press the mixture into a greased 7-inch pie pan to cover the bottom and sides. Bake for 10 minutes.

Peel and finely chop the onion. Simmer in ¼ cup of the vegetable bouillon, uncovered, until the liquid has evaporated and the onion is soft. Reduce the heat and continue to cook for another minute or two, until the onion begins to color. Stir in the flour, then stir in the remaining bouillon and remove from the heat. Let cool slightly. Chop the chives. Beat the egg and add to the cooled bouillon with the mustard, yogurt, chives, and seasoning. Mix well. Spoon into the pie pan and return to the oven to bake for 15 minutes. Serve warm with a crisp green salad.

## 233 Golden baked okra

Serves 4

### Ingredients
- 1 pound okra
- 2 red bell peppers
- 1 onion
- 2 tablespoons vegetable oil
- 4 large eggs
- 2 teaspoons dried mixed herbs
- 5 ounces Cheddar cheese

### Preparation
Preheat the oven to 325°F.

Trim the okra and de-seed and chop the peppers. Peel and chop the onion. Gently sauté the okra, onion, and peppers in the oil for up to eight minutes, until all the vegetables are soft.

Beat the eggs with the dried herbs. Shred the Cheddar cheese and add to the eggs, mixing well. Combine the egg mixture with the cooked vegetables and spoon into a greased baking dish. Bake for 20 minutes, until cooked through, and puffy and golden.

*This country-style recipe can be assembled in advance and slipped into the oven when you get home.*

## 234 Fall root vegetables glazed in cider

Serves 4

### Ingredients

- 2 pounds carrots, parsnips, turnips, sweet potatoes, celery root, beets or other root vegetables
- 1 inch stem or crystallized ginger
- 3 tablespoons salted butter
- ⅓ cup apple cider, juice or hard cider
- 3 tablespoons honey or maple syrup
- Salt and freshly ground black pepper
- Small handful fresh parsley

### Preparation

Preheat the oven to 400°F.

Peel the root vegetables and chop into matchsticks. Finely chop the ginger.

Put the butter, cider, honey, and ginger in a large, shallow baking dish and put into the oven to melt the butter. Remove, and stir to combine the ingredients. Add the prepared root vegetables to the dish, season, and stir well to coat with the cider mixture. Cover with aluminum foil and bake for 30 minutes, then remove the foil, stir the vegetables and return to the oven. Bake for 20 minutes longer, or until the vegetables are tender. Chop the parsley and sprinkle over before serving.

*This moist and colorful side dish works well with nutty casseroles or veggie burgers and baked potatoes.*

## 235 Easy fall risotto

Serves 4

### Ingredients

- 1 clove garlic
- 1 small onion
- ½ pound butternut squash
- ¼ stick salted butter or vegan margarine
- ⅔ cup Arborio rice
- 1 tablespoon mixed herbs
- 1 ¼ cups vegetable bouillon
- ¾ cup white wine
- Salt and freshly ground black pepper

### Preparation

Preheat the oven to 350°F. Crush the garlic. Chop the onion. Peel and cube the butternut squash.

Put the butter and crushed garlic into a baking dish and put in the oven for two minutes, to melt. Add the chopped vegetables and return to the oven for five minutes. Stir in the rice, herbs, bouillon, and wine and return to the oven for 40 minutes, stirring occasionally. Season to taste.

## 236 Leek, mint, and feta terrine

Serves 4

### Ingredients

- 2 ¼ pounds young leeks, no more than 1-inch thick
- Handful fresh mint
- 5 ounces feta cheese
- Salt and freshly ground black pepper

### Preparation

Line a 1-pound loaf pan with several layers of plastic wrap, letting it drape over the sides. Trim the leeks so that they fit neatly along the length of the pan, rinse thoroughly and then boil them in salted water for about 10 minutes, until soft. Drain, and arrange some of the leeks in one layer in the base of the prepared pan.

Chop the mint and crumble the feta. Sprinkle over the top of the leeks and season with salt and pepper. Continue building up the layers, ending with a layer of leeks, pressing down firmly so that the pan is well packed.

Wrap the flaps of plastic wrap over the top of the terrine and weigh it down with another loaf pan filled with some kitchen weights or food cans. Refrigerate for three hours or overnight. To serve, carefully unwrap the terrine onto a chopping board. Slice slowly and carefully using a sharp, serrated knife and a gentle sawing motion.

*Serve cold with a simple vinaigrette or a light mustard sauce.*

## 237 Lemon millet with adzuki beans and corn

Serves 4

### Ingredients

- 1 cup millet
- ½ red onion
- Small handful fresh parsley
- ½ cup canned adzuki or pinto beans
- ¼ cup corn kernels

### For the dressing

- Zest and juice ½ lemon
- 2 tablespoons olive oil
- ½ teaspoon ground coriander
- Freshly ground black pepper

### Preparation

Toast the millet in a dry pan for three minutes. Add 2 cups of water, bring to a boil and then simmer, covered, for around 25 minutes or until all the water has been absorbed and the millet is tender. Set aside to cool.

Make the dressing by mixing together all of the ingredients. Finely chop the red onion and the parsley. Fluff up the cooled millet and stir in the adzuki beans, finely chopped onion, corn, parsley, and dressing. Serve chilled.

## 238 Eggplant and mozzarella casserole

Serves 6

### Ingredients
- 4 eggplants
- ½ pound mozzarella cheese
- 4 ounces strong Cheddar cheese
- ⅓ cup olive oil

### For the sauce
- 2 onions
- 4 cloves garlic
- 2 tablespoons olive oil
- 4 x 15-ounce cans diced tomatoes
- 1 bay leaf
- 1 teaspoon brown sugar
- Salt and freshly ground black pepper

### Preparation
Preheat the oven to 350°F.

Make the tomato sauce first. Peel and finely chop the onions. Peel and chop the garlic. Sauté the onions and garlic in the olive oil until translucent, add the tomatoes and bay leaf, and simmer, stirring frequently, for 25 minutes, until thickened. Add the sugar and season to taste. Remove and discard the bay leaf.

Slice the eggplants lengthwise into slices around ¼ inch thick. Tear the mozzarella into pieces and shred the Cheddar cheese. Sauté the eggplant in small batches, using the olive oil as required, until slightly colored and soft. Layer the slices with the tomato sauce and cheeses in a 13 x 9 x 2-inch baking dish, beginning with eggplant and ending with a layer of cheese. Bake for up to 40 minutes, until golden and bubbling.

## 239 Savory apple fritters

Makes 8

### Ingredients

- ¾ cup all-purpose flour
- 2 large eggs
- 1 tablespoon 2% milk
- 2 large Granny Smith apples
- 4 ounces Cheddar cheese
- ½ pound mozzarella cheese
- Few sprigs fresh thyme
- Salt and freshly ground black pepper
- ¼ cup vegetable oil, to fry

### Preparation

Mix the flour, eggs, and milk to make a thick batter. Shred the apples and Cheddar cheese, and cut up the mozzarella. Strip the thyme leaves from their stalks and chop. Stir into the batter, along with all the remaining ingredients except the oil. Mix thoroughly, and shape into small patties using extra flour to coat.

Pan-fry in small batches until crisp and golden, about one minute each side. Serve hot with the spiced Red Onion Marmalade (see right).

## 240 Red onion marmalade with cinnamon

Serves 4

### Ingredients

- 2 ounces salted butter
- 7 ounces red onions
- 1 large Granny Smith apple
- 3 tablespoons red wine vinegar
- 1 tablespoon brown sugar
- 1 teaspoon ground cinnamon

### Preparation

Melt the butter in a pan. Peel and slice the onions and gently sauté until meltingly soft.

Peel, core, and finely chop the apple. Add to the pan with the vinegar, sugar, and cinnamon, and simmer, uncovered, for 25 minutes. Serve warm or cold.

*Try serving this chutney with the Carrot and Chili Pepper Pancakes on the opposite page or the Savory Apple Fritters, left.*

## 241 Carrot and chili pepper pancakes

Makes 12

### Ingredients

- 2 large eggs
- 1 cup all-purpose flour
- ⅔ cup 2% milk
- 5 ounces carrots
- 1 green chili pepper
- 1 teaspoon cumin seeds
- 3 scallions
- Salt and freshly ground black pepper

### Preparation

Mix the eggs, flour, and milk to make a smooth batter. Finely shred the carrots, de-seed and chop the chili pepper, and stir them in with the remaining ingredients.

Lightly grease a heavy 12-inch skillet and spoon a tablespoon or two of the batter onto the hot surface to make a few pancakes at a time. When the pancakes are dry on top, carefully turn and cook for another minute or two before transferring to a warm plate. Serve warm, with a spicy salsa, warm apple or cranberry sauce, or Red Onion Marmalade (see left).

## 242 Sweet-and-sour tofu

Serves 4

### Ingredients

- 9 ounces firm tofu
- 2 tablespoons vegetable oil
- ¼ cup rice vinegar
- ⅔ cup pineapple juice
- 3 tablespoons brown sugar
- 1 tablespoon cornstarch
- 1 inch ginger root
- 4 ounces pineapple chunks or pieces

### Preparation

Drain the tofu and cut into slices or triangles. Gently sauté in the oil, turning carefully until golden on both sides. Turn onto paper towels to drain.

In a saucepan away from the heat, beat the vinegar, pineapple juice, sugar, and cornstarch together with 4 tablespoons of cold water. Shred the ginger, then gather up all the gratings and squeeze out the juice. Add the ginger juice to the pan, discarding the pulp. Heat the mixture gently until boiling point is reached, beating constantly. Stir in the pineapple pieces and tofu, and heat through, stirring gently, before serving.

# 243 Baked acorn squash

Serves 4

### Ingredients

- 1 acorn squash
- Olive oil, for brushing
- 4 leeks
- 6 ounces cherry tomatoes
- 2 large eggs
- 7 ounces Cheddar cheese
- Salt and freshly ground black pepper
- Small handful fresh basil

### Preparation

Preheat the oven to 425°F.

Cut the squash in half from top to bottom. Scoop out and discard the seeds. Place cut-side down on a baking sheet lined with parchment paper, and bake for 10 minutes. Cut out and reserve the flesh, leaving a shell about ¾ inch thick. Brush the inside of the squash with a little olive oil, return to the baking sheet, and bake for a further five minutes.

Trim and slice the leeks thinly, cut the tomatoes into halves, and chop the reserved squash flesh into bite-size pieces before adding to a large bowl. Beat the eggs, shred the cheese, and mix with the vegetables. Season generously.

Pile the stuffing mixture into the squash shells, cover with aluminum foil and return to the oven for 30 minutes. Remove the foil and cook for a further 15 minutes or so, until browned and bubbling. Tear the fresh basil and sprinkle over the top of the squash before serving.

# 244 Spaghetti baked in parchment

Serves 6

### Ingredients
- 1 pound spaghetti
- 4 cloves garlic
- Small handful fresh, flat-leaf parsley
- ¼ cup olive oil
- 2 teaspoons dried red pepper flakes
- Sea salt flakes and freshly ground black pepper
- ⅓ cup dry white wine

### Preparation
Preheat the oven to 375°F.

Cook the spaghetti in salted, boiling water until just tender, drain and rinse with cold water.

Peel and crush the garlic and chop the parsley. Warm the oil in a small pan and sauté the garlic and red pepper flakes together for a minute or two. Remove from the heat and stir in the parsley, salt and pepper. In a large bowl, mix together the cooked spaghetti, garlic oil, and white wine. Toss until well combined.

Divide the spaghetti between six large squares of parchment paper and fold the paper around the pasta to form parcels. Put on a baking sheet and bake for 15 minutes. Put each parcel on a serving plate and let guests open with care.

*An unusual way to present a very simple dish! Serve with small bowls of pitted black olives, shredded cheese, chopped sun-dried tomatoes, toasted pine nuts, and capers, for guests to help themselves.*

## 245 Mushroom and sage sausages

Serves 4

### Ingredients

- 1 large onion
- 1 tablespoon vegetable oil
- 7 ounces whole-wheat bread
- Handful fresh sage leaves
- ½ pound button mushrooms
- 1 large egg
- 1 ½ cups ground almonds
- Salt and freshly ground black pepper

### Preparation

Finely chop the onion and sauté in the oil until transparent. Put the bread and sage in a food processor and pulse to fine crumbs. Wipe and finely chop the mushrooms. Add to the bread crumbs and pulse until well combined.

Beat the egg. Transfer the mushroom mixture to a large mixing bowl and stir in the cooked onion, ground almonds, beaten egg, and seasoning. Shape the mixture into six or eight thick sausages and chill for at least 30 minutes.

Sauté the sausages gently in a little vegetable oil, or brush them with oil, put on a parchment paper-lined baking sheet and bake at 400°F for 25 minutes, until brown.

*These sausages are good served in warmed bread rolls with corn relish or mustard and ketchup.*

## 246 Leek and Cheddar sausages

Serves 4

### Ingredients

- 2 leeks
- 5 ounces strong Cheddar cheese
- 3 tablespoons vegetable oil
- 6 cups fresh white bread crumbs
- 1 tablespoon wholegrain mustard
- 3 large eggs
- Salt and freshly ground black pepper

### Preparation

Wash and chop the leeks and shred the cheese. Cook the leeks in 1 tablespoon of the vegetable oil until softened. Transfer to a large bowl, and mix in 4 cups of the bread crumbs, the shredded cheese, mustard, and 2 of the eggs. Season and chill for 30 minutes.

Beat the remaining egg and place it in a shallow dish. Put the remaining bread crumbs on a large plate next to it and season with salt and freshly ground black pepper. Shape the sausage mixture into eight sausages, dip into the beaten egg, then roll in the bread crumbs until well coated. Gently sauté the sausages in the oil for 10 minutes, until golden.

# 247 Hearty vegetarian sausage and cider casserole

Serves 4

### Ingredients

- 1 pound potatoes
- 1 large onion
- Few sprigs fresh thyme
- 3 tablespoons vegetable oil
- 1 large Granny Smith apple
- 1 large carrot
- 1 x 15-ounce can diced tomatoes
- 1 tablespoon tomato paste
- 2 ½ cups vegetable bouillon
- 6 vegetarian sausages
- ⅓ cup apple cider, juice or hard cider

### Preparation

Peel the potatoes and parboil in a 2-quart pan. Cut into small chunks, then parboil again for two minutes. Drain. Chop the onion. Strip the thyme leaves from the stalks and chop. Sauté the onion in the oil until beginning to brown, then stir in the thyme. Peel, core, and cube the apple, peel and dice the carrot and add both to the pan.

Transfer to a 3-quart pan and add the tomatoes, tomato paste, bouillon, and potatoes. Bring to a boil, then simmer until the potatoes and carrots are cooked through, about 10 minutes. Cook the vegetarian sausages and cut into chunks. Stir the apple cider into the pan and cook for another three minutes, then stir in the vegetarian sausage pieces and warm through before serving.

# 248 Sweet potato and okra casserole

Serves 4

### Ingredients

- 1 ½ pounds sweet potatoes
- 6 ounces okra
- 1 onion
- 1 red chili pepper
- 1 inch ginger root
- 1 tablespoon vegetable oil
- 2 ½ cups vegetable bouillon
- 2 teaspoons cinnamon
- 1 x 15-ounce can diced tomatoes
- Small handful fresh cilantro

### Preparation

Peel the sweet potatoes and cut them into bite-size pieces. Trim the okra and cut into small chunks. Peel and roughly chop the onion. De-seed and finely chop the chili pepper. Shred the ginger root.

Warm the vegetable oil in a flameproof casserole dish and sauté the onions gently until they are soft and translucent. Stir in the chili pepper, ginger, and cinnamon and cook for a further minute. Stir in the sweet potatoes and bouillon, and simmer for five minutes, until the potatoes begin to soften. Add the diced tomatoes and okra, stir together well, cover, and simmer for a further 15 minutes or so, until all the vegetables are tender. Chop the cilantro and sprinkle over the casserole before serving.

# 249 Green tomato chutney with cumin

Serves 4

### Ingredients
- 3 pounds small green tomatoes
- 3 cups white wine vinegar
- 2 pounds sugar
- ½ teaspoon ground cumin

### Preparation

Drop the whole tomatoes in a 3-quart pan or bowl of boiling water, prick each one with the tip of a sharp knife and leave for one minute. Drain and transfer to a bowl of ice-cold water. The skins should split and the tomatoes will then be easy to peel. Put the peeled tomatoes into a 3-quart pan with the vinegar, sugar, and cumin, and boil rapidly for five minutes.

To preserve the chutney, transfer it while still hot to sterilized jars and seal immediately. The seal will tighten as the chutney cools. Alternatively, the chutney can be stored in a jar or covered bowl in the refrigerator for a week.

*Don't let those unripened tomatoes go to waste! This simple preserve works well with cheese and in sandwiches made with nut or bean pâtés. This is a perfect way to use up the last of the tomato crop—it works well with red or yellow tomatoes, too, and makes sure that nothing goes to waste.*

# 250 Blackberry jelly

Serves 4

### Ingredients
- 3 pounds blackberries
- 2 large Granny Smith apples
- 2 cups water
- Juice 1 lemon
- Sugar (see below for amount)

### Preparation
Wash the blackberries for cobwebs and insects. Wash the apples, then skin, core and chop them. Bring the water to a boil in a 4-quart pan, add the blackberries, apple pieces and lemon juice and simmer for 20 minutes, until the fruit is soft.

Transfer the fruit and juice into a sterilized jelly bag suspended over a large bowl and leave it to drip overnight. A colander lined with washed cheesecloth can also be used. Be patient and don't be tempted to squeeze the bag, because this will make the jelly cloudy.

Measure the juice in a cup and then return it to a preserving or 6-quart pan. For every 2½ cups of juice add 1 pound of sugar. Bring to a boil and simmer for up to 15 minutes, spooning away any bubbly residue that forms.

To test for setting, chill a small plate. Put a spoonful of the hot jelly mixture onto the plate and place in the refrigerator for five minutes. Now push the edge of the jelly with your finger—if it wrinkles, setting point has been reached.

Carefully pour the hot liquid into sterilized jars, seal and store in a cool, dark place.

*This jelly is not just for breakfast or sweet dishes, it is delicious with cheese and crackers too!*

## 251 Mulled apple juice

Serves 4

**Ingredients**
- 1 large orange
- 1 quart apple juice
- 2 cinnamon sticks
- 5 cloves
- Honey, to taste

**Preparation**

Using a vegetable peeler or sharp knife, remove the zest of the orange in thick strips. Juice the orange.

Gently warm the apple juice, orange juice and zest, cinnamon, and cloves in a pan for 10 minutes. Sweeten with honey to taste.

## 252 Pear and ginger zinger

Serves 4

**Ingredients**
- 3 firm pears
- 1 inch ginger root
- Juice ½ lemon
- Sparkling mineral water, to taste

**Preparation**

Juice the pears and the ginger. Add the lemon juice and dilute to taste with sparkling mineral water.

*Best consumed immediately after making, this is a wonderfully refreshing breakfast juice.*

## 253 Honey banana smoothie

Serves 4

### Ingredients
- 1 ripe banana
- 1½ cups 2% milk
  or non-dairy alternative
- 1 to 2 tablespoons honey
  or maple syrup
- ¼ teaspoon ground nutmeg
- 3 ice cubes

### Preparation
Put all the ingredients in a blender and blend until smooth. Serve immediately as a satisfying breakfast. Alternatively, omit the ice cubes and add a little more milk to the blended mixture. Transfer to a saucepan, warm gently and serve in heatproof glasses topped with a sprinkle of freshly ground nutmeg.

## 254 Almond chocolate milk

Serves 4

### Ingredients
- 2 cups almonds
- 6 cups cold water
- 3 dried dates
- 2 teaspoons carob or cocoa powder

### Preparation
Working in batches, put the nuts and water in a blender and blend on high speed for several minutes. Combine and strain the mixture through two layers of muslin. Return the "milk" to the blender and blend in the dates and carob or cocoa powder.

*A healthy vegan alternative to a chocolate milkshake, sweetened with dates. This is always a hit with children!*

# 255 Poached pears with hot chocolate sauce

Serves 4

## Ingredients

- 1 vanilla bean
- 1 ¼ cups white or sweet wine
- ¼ cup sugar
- 2 tablespoons honey
- 1 cinnamon stick
- 4 pears
- 1 pound semi-sweet chocolate
- ¾ stick unsalted butter

## Preparation

Split the vanilla bean. Put the white wine, sugar, honey, cinnamon stick, and split vanilla bean in a deep saucepan and heat to a gentle simmer. Carefully immerse the pears in the liquid. Poach over a low heat for 30 minutes, or until translucent, turning occasionally. Remove the pears from the pan, turn up the heat and continue to cook the liquid to make a pourable syrup.

Break up the chocolate and melt with the butter in a heatproof bowl over a saucepan of simmering water. When the mixture is smooth remove from the heat, but leave the bowl on the warm pan so that the sauce does not cool and set. Serve each pear on a pool of warm syrup, topped with the warm chocolate sauce.

*A little vanilla ice cream is a lovely addition to this dish.*

# 256 Apple and fig mille-feuille

Serves 6

## Ingredients

- 1 lemon
- 5 medium Granny Smith apples
- ½ pound dried figs
- 1 cup apple cider
- ¼ cup sugar
- 1 teaspoon cinnamon
- 1 package phyllo pastry
- 3 teaspoons confectioners' sugar
- Vegetable oil, for brushing

*Made with layers of pastry, this is a classic pâtisserie. Mille feuille means "thousand leaves" in French.*

## Preparation

Preheat the oven to 400°F.

Using a vegetable peeler, peel the zest from the lemon in wide strips. Squeeze half the lemon. Peel and core the apples and cut into large chunks. Chop the figs.

In a 3-quart pan, mix together the lemon peel and juice, apple chunks, cider, chopped figs, sugar, and cinnamon. Cover and heat to boiling point, then reduce the heat and simmer, covered, for around 10 minutes, until the apples are just tender. Remove from the heat and let cool.

Separate one sheet of the phyllo pastry and lay it on a floured board. Brush it lightly with vegetable oil, and lay another sheet on top. Repeat to make a stack of four sheets of pastry. Using a sharp knife, carefully cut the stack of pastry sheets lengthwise into three equal strips. Then cut each strip into six equal rectangles.

Transfer the pastry stacks to a baking sheet lined with parchment paper and bake for up to eight minutes, until crisp and golden. Remove from the oven and transfer the cooked pastry pieces to a cooling rack.

Assemble the mille-feuille immediately before serving. Place one pastry piece on a serving plate and top with the apple and fig mixture. Put a second pastry piece on top of that and add more of the fruit. Finish with a final pastry piece and sprinkle with confectioners' sugar and a little more cinnamon to serve. Repeat with the remaining fruit mixture and pastry pieces until you have six mille-feuille towers.

## 257 Banana chocolate muffins

Makes 12

### Ingredients
- ¾ cup unsalted butter
- 1 tablespoon honey
- 2 ripe bananas
- 2 cups all-purpose flour
- 1 teaspoon baking powder
- ½ teaspoon baking soda
- Pinch salt
- Pinch nutmeg
- ½ cup brown sugar
- 3 ounces semi-sweet chocolate
- 2 large eggs
- ½ cup milk

### Preparation
Preheat the oven to 375°F. Grease a muffin pan or line with paper or silicone baking cups.

Melt the butter, stir in the honey and set to one side to cool slightly. Mash the bananas. Sift the flour, baking powder, baking soda, salt, and nutmeg into a large mixing bowl. Add the sugar and chocolate in chunks, and mix well.

Beat the eggs with the milk, and add the cooled melted butter and honey. Stir in the mashed bananas. Stir the dry and wet mixtures together until just combined.

Divide the batter between the muffin cups and bake for 20 minutes, or until well risen and cooked through. Let cool for five minutes in the pan before transferring to a cooling rack.

## 258 Crunchy pear and cinnamon muffins

Makes 12

### Ingredients
- 1 ¾ cups all-purpose flour
- 2 teaspoons baking powder
- ⅔ cup soft brown sugar
- ½ teaspoon salt
- 3 teaspoons cinnamon
- 1 large egg
- ¼ cup vegetable oil
- ¼ cup 2% milk
- 2 pears
- 1 tablespoon pecans or walnuts
- 2 tablespoons turbinado sugar

### Preparation
Preheat the oven to 400° F. Grease a muffin pan or line with paper or silicone baking cups.

Sift the flour and baking powder together into a large mixing bowl, and stir in the sugar, salt, and 2 teaspoons of the cinnamon. Beat the egg with the oil and milk. Pour into the flour and mix until just combined. Peel and chop the pears and fold in. Spoon the batter into the prepared muffin cups.

Chop or crush the nuts and mix into the turbinado sugar and remaining cinnamon. Sprinkle over the muffins. Bake for 20 minutes, or until well risen and cooked through.

# 259 Black cherry and chocolate puffs

Makes 18

## Ingredients

- 1 package puff pastry sheets
- 2 cups heavy cream
- 1 teaspoon vanilla extract
- ¼ cup confectioners' sugar
- Juice 1 lemon
- 3 ounces semi-sweet chocolate
- 3 tablespoons boiling water
- 30 pitted black cherries, fresh or canned

## Preparation

Preheat the oven to 350°F.

Using a sharp knife, cut the pastry lengthwise into three equal strips. Then cut each strip into six equal pieces. Transfer the pastry pieces to a baking sheet lined with parchment paper and bake for 15 minutes, or until puffy and golden. Transfer to a wire rack to cool.

Whip the cream together with the vanilla extract. To make the frosting, mix the confectioners' sugar with enough lemon juice and warm water so it is runny. Break up the chocolate and melt in a heatproof bowl above a small pan of simmering water. Beat in the 3 tablespoons of boiling water until thoroughly combined. Halve the cherries.

To assemble the puffs, carefully slice each piece of pastry in half, horizontally. Brush the bottom layer pieces with a little lemon frosting, then spoon on some whipped cream and melted chocolate. Press a few cherry pieces into the chocolate and cream. Cover with the pastry tops and drizzle with melted chocolate and lemon frosting.

# Five ways with apples

## 260
### Baked
Core apples and stuff with dried fruit soaked in brandy and unsalted butter. Place in an oven dish, cover loosely with foil and bake at 300°F for an hour, uncovering for the last 20 minutes.

## 261
### Sauce
Peel and chop Granny Smith apples, then cook in a little water until soft. Add sweeteners (honey, brown sugar, maple syrup) and spices (cinnamon, allspice, nutmeg, cloves) to taste.

## 262
### Soup
Apples lend a subtle sweetness to soups made with root vegetables such as celery root, carrots, parsnips, or beets. Sauté them with the vegetables, add vegetable bouillon and blend.

## 263
### Salad
The classic Waldorf salad is made with apples, walnuts, and celery tossed in mayonnaise, but apples can also work well with fennel, beets, and cabbage. Apple juice can also be used in salad dressing, blended with oil and finely chopped shallots.

## 264
### Juice
Apple and carrot juice is the classic "starter" when experimenting with juicing. Try juicing a little ginger root with the mixture, or add a splash of freshly squeezed lemon juice.

# 265 Vegan raspberry muffins
Makes 12

**Ingredients**

- 1 cup soy milk
- 1 tablespoon apple cider vinegar
- 2 ½ cups all-purpose flour
- 1 ½ teaspoons baking powder
- 1 teaspoon baking soda
- ½ teaspoon salt
- ¾ cup sugar
- ⅓ cup unsweetened apple sauce
- 1 teaspoon vanilla extract
- 4 ounces raspberries

**Preparation**

Preheat the oven to 375°F. Grease a muffin pan or line with paper or silicone baking liners.

Mix the soy milk with the vinegar and leave to one side for five minutes to curdle. Sift the flour, baking powder, baking soda, and salt into a large mixing bowl, and stir in the sugar. Add the apple sauce and vanilla extract to the curdled soy milk, and then pour the wet ingredients over the dry ingredients and stir until just combined. Gently fold in the raspberries. Divide the mixture between the muffin cups and bake for 20 minutes.

## 266 Pear custard

Serves 4

### Ingredients

- Butter, for greasing
- 4 ripe pears
- 1 ½ cups all-purpose flour
- ¾ cup sugar, plus 2 tablespoons
- 4 large eggs
- 2 cups half and half
- Maple syrup, to serve

### Preparation

Preheat the oven to 375°F.

Peel, quarter and core the pears and arrange them in the base of a greased baking dish.

In a large bowl, mix the flour and sugar together (reserving 2 tablespoons sugar) then beat in the eggs and the half and half. Pour over the pears and sprinkle with the reserved sugar. Bake for 45 minutes, until golden. Serve topped with a little maple syrup.

## 267 Blackberry and apple crumble

Serves 4

### Ingredients

- 1 pound Granny Smith apples
- 10 ounces blackberries
- ½ cup sugar
- ½ teaspoon ground allspice
- 1 ¼ cups all-purpose flour
- ¾ stick unsalted butter
- ⅓ cup chopped toasted hazelnuts
- 3 tablespoons brown sugar

### Preparation

Preheat the oven to 375°F.

Peel, core, and slice the apples, and arrange them in the base of a greased baking dish with the blackberries. Sprinkle on the sugar and allspice.

Put the flour into a large bowl, blend the butter and then stir in the nuts and brown sugar. Cover the fruit with the crumble topping, pressing down gently to make a firm layer. Bake for 30 minutes, until golden and crisp.

# 268 Apple and almond cake

Serves 6

## Ingredients

- 4 apples
- ¼ stick unsalted butter
- 2 tablespoons brown sugar
- 1 teaspoon ground cinnamon

### For the cake

- 1 ¼ sticks unsalted butter
- ½ cup sugar
- 2 large eggs
- 1 teaspoon almond extract
- ½ cup plus 2 tablespoons
  self-rising flour
- ⅔ cup ground almonds

## Preparation

Preheat the oven to 325°F. Grease an
8-inch baking pan and line the base with
parchment paper.

Peel, core, and slice the apples. Melt the
butter in a skillet, stir in the sugar and
keep stirring until the mixture bubbles.
Add the sliced apples and cinnamon and
cook gently, turning occasionally, until
tender and slightly caramelized. Remove
from the heat.

For the cake, beat the butter and sugar
together in a large bowl until light and
fluffy, then gradually beat in the eggs and
almond extract. Gently fold in the flour and
ground almonds, and spoon the mixture
into the prepared pan. Smooth the surface
and arrange the cooked apples on top. Pour
any juice left in the skillet over the batter.

Bake for 45 minutes, using a skewer to
check that it is cooked through. Before
removing the cake from the pan, let cool for
a few minutes.

*Serve this cake warm with whipped cream
or Greek yogurt.*

# Five ways with nuts

## 269
### Breakfast energy
Enjoy an energizing raw-food breakfast of hazelnuts and pecans, dates or dried apricots, golden raisins, and fresh seasonal fruit. Chop together and moisten with fruit juice or nut milk.

## 270
### Nut milk
Make a dairy alternative by blending cashews, macadamias, or almonds with cold water in a blender. Strain through muslin or a nut milk bag, and sweeten with maple syrup or agave nectar.

## 271
### Spiced nuts
Toss whole, blanched almonds with a little vegetable oil, sprinkle with ground cumin and coriander, and bake for 10 minutes in a medium-heat oven until crisp.

## 272
### Sweet treat
Coat pecans, macadamias and Brazil nuts with a mixture of beaten egg white, sugar, and spices such as cinnamon, ground ginger, or cloves, and bake at 300°F for 45 minutes.

## 273
### Pesto
Walnuts, cashews, and pecans all work well for pestos—sticking to a single variety will give the best flavor. Use a blender or a pestle and mortar, and grind to a paste with basil, parsley, or cilantro, and olive oil and sea salt.

# 274 Vegan vanilla cupcakes

Makes 12

### Ingredients

- 1 teaspoon cider vinegar
- 2 cups soy milk
- ¼ cup canola oil
- 2 teaspoons vanilla extract
- 1¼ cups sugar
- 1¾ cups all-purpose flour
- 2 tablespoons cornstarch
- ¾ teaspoon baking powder
- ½ teaspoon baking soda
- ½ teaspoon salt

### For the icing

- 1 cup margarine
- 2¼ cups confectioners' sugar
- ½ teaspoon vanilla extract
- 1½ tablespoons soy milk

### Preparation

Preheat the oven to 350°F. Grease a cupcake pan or line with paper or silicone baking liners.

Mix the vinegar and soy milk together and set it aside for five minutes to curdle. Stir in the oil, sugar, and vanilla extract. Sift the flour, cornstarch, baking powder, baking soda, and salt together. Combine the wet and dry ingredients and mix to a smooth batter. Divide the mixture between the baking cups or cupcake pan, and bake for 20 minutes, or until cooked through and golden. Transfer the cupcakes to a wire rack to cool before frosting.

To make the frosting, cream all the ingredients together well. Use a spatula or a pastry bag to frost the cakes.

# 275 Baked berry cheesecake

Serves 8

## Ingredients
- 10 graham crackers
- ½ stick unsalted butter
- 1¼ pounds cream cheese
- 2 tablespoons all-purpose flour
- ¾ cup sugar
- 2 large eggs plus 1 egg yolk
- ⅔ cup sour cream
- 2 to 3 drops vanilla extract
- 5 ounces mixed raspberries, blackberries, or other berries

## For the sauce
- 5 ounces mixed blackberries, raspberries, blueberries, or other berries
- 2 tablespoons confectioners' sugar

## Preparation

Preheat the oven to 350°F.

Crush the crackers and melt the butter. Mix the cracker crumbs and butter together and spread over the base of a greased 8-inch spring-form or removable bottom baking pan, pressing down firmly. Bake for five minutes, then set aside.

Beat the cream cheese, flour, sugar, eggs and egg yolk, sour cream, and vanilla extract together until well combined. Gently stir in the berries and pour over the cheesecake base. Smooth the top and bake for 45 minutes until set. Let cool in the pan before removing.

To make the sauce, rinse the berries and put them into a saucepan with the sugar. Warm gently, stirring occasionally until the berries collapse and release their juice. Push through a sieve and discard the pulp. Serve the sauce with the cheesecake as an optional extra!

# 276 Raspberry clafoutis

Serves 6

### Ingredients

- 3 tablespoons all-purpose flour
- Pinch salt
- 3 tablespoons sugar
- 3 large eggs
- 1 ¼ cups 2% milk
- 1 tablespoon oil
- 1 tablespoon unsalted butter for greasing
- ½ pound raspberries
- Confectioners' sugar, to garnish

### Preparation

Heat the oven to 350°F.

Put the flour, salt, and sugar into a big bowl. In another bowl beat the eggs, milk, and oil together, then beat into the other ingredients to make a smooth batter. Grease a deep 8-inch baking dish and line it with parchment paper. Put the raspberries in the dish and carefully pour over the batter.

Bake for 45 minutes, then reduce the oven temperature to 300°F and cook for a further 30 minutes. Test whether the clafoutis is cooked by inserting the tip of a knife or a skewer. It should come out clean. Remove from the oven and allow the clafoutis to stand for an hour and then serve straight from the dish, sprinkled with confectioners' sugar.

# Winter

## Soups, salads, and appetizers

## Mains and sides

## Drinks and sweets

# Fresh in Season ...

### Parsnips

Giant parsnips are impressive to look at but can be woody inside—choose medium-size, firm specimens for cooking or cut out the dense core. Peel, boil, and mash them, or blanch and roast them, as you would potatoes.

### Sweet potatoes

Look for medium-sized roots with good uniform color and no soft spots. Sweet potatoes should be peeled and roasted or boiled—large ones are good baked in their skins and served with butter or vegan mayonnaise.

### Celery root

This large, dense root is a relative of celery and has a distinctive, subtle celery flavor. Don't worry about the lumpy exterior, just peel it with a potato peeler, cut it into chunks and try it boiled, roasted, or mashed. Note that this vegetable is also sometimes called celeriac.

### Cauliflower

Look for cauliflowers with pure white "curds" protected by crisp green outer leaves. They're not just for baking in cheese sauce—their subtle flavor works well with curries, or try individual florets deep fried in tempura batter.

### Red cabbage

Choose medium-sized, firm cabbages, and peel away the outermost leaves before using. Shredded red cabbage adds color and texture to winter salads, and is also popular when baked slowly with apples and served as a side dish.

### Kohlrabi

Also called turnip-rooted cabbage, there are green and purple varieties. Look for small young specimens that are crisp and tender—they can be shredded or sliced and eaten raw, or stir-fried. More mature specimens are best steamed and then peeled.

### Kale

Kale's dark green crinkly leaves can be cooked like cabbage (cut out any really tough-looking "ribs"), but it is also good raw. Shred it finely, add a citrus salad dressing and use your hands to squash and squeeze the salad before serving.

### Brussels sprouts

Look for small, firm buds without many yellow leaves. Remove one or two outer leaves and if the base is thick, cut a cross in the bottom to help it cook more quickly. Boil until tender but not soggy, or shred and stir-fry.

## 277 Tomato and red lentil soup

Serves 4

### Ingredients

- 2 onions
- Few sprigs fresh marjoram
- Small handful fresh parsley
- 2 tablespoons olive oil
- 5 cups vegetable bouillon
- 2 x 15-ounce cans diced tomatoes
- 1 cup red lentils
- Salt and freshly ground black pepper

### Preparation

Peel the onions and chop them roughly. Strip the marjoram leaves away from the woody stems and chop them finely along with the parsley. In a 4-quart heavy pan, sauté the chopped onions in the olive oil until softened. Pour in the bouillon and add the diced tomatoes and lentils.

Simmer, covered, for up to 40 minutes, until the lentils are completely soft. Let cool a little, transfer to a blender, and blend until smooth. Return to the saucepan, reheat and stir in the fresh herbs. Season with salt and pepper before serving.

*This attractive orange soup looks lovely topped with a pool of green pesto. Look for a brand that uses vegetarian cheese—or better still, make your own!*

## 278 Parsnip and apple soup

Serves 4

### Ingredients

- 1 ¾ pounds parsnips
- 1 large Granny Smith apple
- 1 sprig fresh sage
- ¼ stick salted butter
- 5 cups vegetable bouillon
- 2 cloves
- ½ cup half and half
- Salt and freshly ground black pepper

### Preparation

Peel the parsnips, and peel and core the apple. Chop both into small pieces. Finely chop the sage. In a 4-quart heavy pan, sauté the parsnips and apple in the butter until soft. Pour in the bouillon and add the sage and cloves. Simmer, covered, for 20 minutes. Let cool slightly and remove the clove before transferring to a blender and blending until smooth. Before reheating, stir in the half and half, and season with salt and pepper. This smooth, comforting soup is best served with crusty bread.

## 279 Hummus with hot spices

Serves 4

### Ingredients

- 1 x 15-ounce can chickpeas
- 1 clove garlic
- 1 tablespoon tahini
- Juice ½ lemon
- 1 tablespoon olive oil
- ½ teaspoon dried red pepper flakes
- ½ teaspoon ground cumin
- ½ teaspoon ground coriander
- Salt and freshly ground black pepper
- 1 teaspoon vegetable oil, for the pan
- ½ teaspoon hot paprika

### Preparation

Drain and rinse the chickpeas, and reserve a tablespoon of them. Peel and crush the garlic. Put the chickpeas in a blender and blend to a soft paste with the tahini, garlic, lemon juice, olive oil, red pepper flakes, cumin, and coriander. Taste and adjust the seasoning with salt and pepper, adding a little more oil, tahini, or lemon juice according to taste if the mixture seems too thick.

Heat the vegetable oil in a skillet and sauté the reserved whole chickpeas for up to three minutes, turning frequently, until they begin to brown. To serve, transfer the hummus to a large shallow bowl and top with the whole chickpeas, a swirl of olive oil and a sprinkle of hot paprika.

## 280 Hot radicchio salad

Serves 4

### Ingredients

- 1 blood orange
- 1 head radicchio
- 1 tablespoon olive oil
- 1 teaspoon caraway seeds
- 1 red chili pepper
- 1 small red onion
- 1 teaspoon cider vinegar
- 1 tablespoon red wine
- 1 tablespoon wholegrain mustard
- 1 teaspoon honey or maple syrup

### Preparation

Shred the zest from the orange and squeeze out the juice. Cut the radicchio into quarters, discard the tough core and separate the leaves. Toss with the orange zest and juice, olive oil, and caraway seeds. De-seed and finely chop the chili pepper. Peel and slice the onion, then marinate with the chopped chili pepper in a mixture of the cider vinegar, red wine, mustard, and honey or maple syrup for at least 15 minutes, or until you are ready to serve the dish.

Stir-fry the radicchio and the onion mixture together in a 4-quart pan or wok on a high heat for five minutes, until the leaves are wilted and the flavors well combined.

## 281 Onion soup
Serves 4

### Ingredients
- 2 pounds onions
- ½ stick salted butter
- 2 tablespoons all-purpose flour
- 2 ½ cups vegetable bouillon
- 3 tablespoons sherry
- Soy sauce, to taste
- Salt and freshly ground black pepper

### Preparation
Peel the onions and slice thinly into rings. In a 3-quart heavy pan, sauté the onions gently in the butter for up to 20 minutes, until they are a rich, golden brown. Stir in the flour and gradually add the warm bouillon, stirring continuously. Stir in the sherry and simmer for 15 minutes. Taste and adjust the seasoning with soy sauce, salt, and pepper. Serve with a bowl of finely shredded vegetarian cheese, so that people can help themselves, or with cheese on toast, cut into fingers.

## 282 Beet consommé
Serves 4

### Ingredients
- 2 pounds beets
- 2 carrots
- 2 turnips
- 5 cups vegetable bouillon
- 2 teaspoons red wine vinegar
- Salt and freshly ground black pepper

### Preparation
Peel the beets, carrots, and turnips, and finely chop. Put them into a 4-quart pan with the bouillon, bring to a boil and simmer, covered, for 45 minutes, until the vegetables are soft.

Strain the soup through a sieve but take care not to press the vegetables—just drain off the clear liquid. If you push the vegetables through, you will end up with muddy consommé! Reheat and season to taste with the vinegar, salt, and pepper.

## 283 Beet and fennel topping

Serves 4

### Ingredients

- 3 beets
- 3 tablespoons olive oil
- Salt and freshly ground black pepper
- 1 fennel bulb
- 1 tablespoon balsamic vinegar
- 1 teaspoon fennel seeds

### Preparation

Preheat the oven to 425°F.

Trim away the beet leaves but do not cut or peel the roots. Put the beets into a bowl and mix with half the olive oil and seasoning. Transfer to a large square of parchment paper, fold into a parcel and wrap the paper parcel in aluminum foil. Roast in the oven for up to 90 minutes, until the beets are tender.

Cut the fennel from top to bottom into ¼ inch slices. Put in a bowl and toss with the remaining olive oil and balsamic vinegar. Transfer to a baking sheet and cook for 20 minutes, until golden but not browned.

Allow the beets to cool a little, then rub off the skins under cold running water. Trim the ends, cut into small dice and put in a bowl. Chop the cooked fennel into small pieces and add to the beets. Crush the fennel seeds and stir into the mixture. Serve warm on blinis or as a side dish.

## 284 Buckwheat blinis

Makes 12

### Ingredients

- ½ cup 2% milk
- ½ package (⅛ ounce) dry yeast
- 1 large egg
- ¾ cup buckwheat or spelt flour
- Pinch salt
- Vegetable oil, for the pan

### Preparation

Warm the milk gently until it is tepid, and divide equally between two small bowls. Dissolve the yeast in one of the bowls of milk and put it in a warm place. Leave to stand for 45 minutes, until the yeast begins to work and bubbles appear on the surface of the mixture.

Separate the egg, beat the yolk into the second bowl of milk, and then transfer both the milk mixtures to a large mixing bowl. Mix in the flour and salt, cover with a damp cloth, and leave in a warm place for an hour. Then beat the egg white to stiff peaks and gently fold in.

Lightly oil a 12-inch heavy skillet and allow it to warm before dropping small spoonfuls of the blini mixture onto the hot surface. Cook gently for up to two minutes on each side, until puffy and golden.

## 285 Winter squash and sage topping

Serves 4

### Ingredients

- 12 ounces winter squash: butternut squash, acorn squash or pumpkin
- Handful fresh sage
- ½ red chili pepper
- 2 tablespoons olive oil
- Salt and freshly ground black pepper
- 1 tablespoon vegetable oil, for the pan

### Preparation

Preheat the oven to 400°F.

Peel the squash and cut it into small cubes. Set aside a few sage leaves for garnish and chop the rest finely. De-seed and chop the chili pepper finely.

Toss the squash pieces with the olive oil, salt, and pepper, transfer to a baking sheet and roast for up to 20 minutes, until tender and beginning to caramelize. Transfer the squash with the cooking oil to a large bowl and mix together with the chopped sage and chili pepper.

Heat the vegetable oil in a skillet and very quickly sauté the sage leaves until they begin to crisp—this only takes about 10 seconds. Remove from the pan with a slotted spoon and let cool on a sheet of kitchen towel.

Top blinis or toasted sourdough bread with a teaspoon or two of the warm squash mixture, and decorate each with a sage leaf.

## 286 Spinach and walnut pâté

Serves 4

### Ingredients

- 1 pound fresh leaf spinach
- 2 cloves garlic
- ½ cup walnut pieces
- 1 teaspoon ground coriander
- 1 teaspoon cayenne pepper
- Small handful fresh parsley
- 1 tablespoon olive oil
- Juice ½ lemon
- Salt and freshly ground black pepper

### Preparation

Wash the spinach and cook it in a little water for five minutes, until wilted. Drain and set aside to cool.

Peel and crush the garlic and put it into a food processor with the walnuts, coriander, cayenne, parsley, and olive oil. Blend to a coarse paste.

When the spinach is cool enough to handle, chop it finely and squeeze out as much water as you can. Add it to the nut mixture in the food processor and blend again, adding lemon juice, salt, and pepper to taste.

*Pâtés look attractive served as quenelles (see photo). The technique involves passing a little of the mixture back and forth between two spoons to make the distinctive shape. It's a nice skill to learn and you can find helpful short videos demonstrating the technique on the Internet.*

## 287 Broccoli and macadamia salad

Serves 4

### Ingredients
- ½ cup canned chickpeas
- 2 cloves garlic
- ½ lemon
- 3 tablespoons olive oil
- ⅓ cup white wine vinegar
- 2 heads broccoli
- 1 cup whole macadamia nuts

### Preparation

Drain and rinse the chickpeas. Peel the garlic cloves and crush them. Shred the zest from the lemon and then squeeze out the juice. Blend together the chickpeas, garlic, lemon zest, olive oil, and vinegar, adding lemon juice as required to make a runny consistency.

Divide the broccoli into individual florets and cut from top to bottom into slices about ¼-inch thick. Toss with the macadamia nuts, transfer to a large shallow bowl and top with the chickpea dressing.

## 288 Celery root, apple, and grape salad

Serves 4

### Ingredients
- 1 celery root
- 2 apples
- 1 cup walnut halves or pieces
- ½ pound green seedless grapes
- Approximately ¾ cup mayonnaise

### Preparation

Peel the celery root using a sharp knife to remove the knobbly brown outer layer. Cut the white flesh into thin slices and then into matchsticks. Blanch the celery root in a 3-quart pan of boiling salted water for 30 seconds. Transfer to a colander and refresh under cold running water.

Slice the apples into matchsticks similar in size and shape to the celery root pieces. Toast the walnut halves in a heavy dry pan for a few minutes. Halve the grapes. Pat the celery root and apple dry with paper towels. Transfer to a bowl with the toasted walnuts and grapes, and stir in sufficient mayonnaise to coat all the fruit, nuts, and vegetables.

# 289 Immune booster salad

Serves 4

**V**

### Ingredients

- ¼ cup pearl barley
- 1 cup wild rice
- 3 cups water
- Pinch salt
- 1 small red onion
- 2 ounces arame seaweed
- 1 tablespoon golden raisins
- 1 tablespoon goji berries
- Juice ½ lemon
- 2 tablespoons flaxseed oil
- 1 tablespoon cider vinegar
- 2 ounces toasted slivered almonds
- ¼ cup toasted sesame seeds

*This powerhouse of a dish is crammed with superfoods to provide a real boost on a cold, dark day. Cider vinegar, goji berries, and sea vegetables add color and texture to a dish of wild rice and barley grains.*

### Preparation

Soak the barley in cold water for one hour. Drain, and place in a 3-quart heavy pan with the wild rice, water, and salt. Bring to a boil, then reduce to a very low heat and cook for approximately 40 minutes, until all the water has been absorbed. Let cool, then fluff with a fork.

Peel and finely chop the onion. Soak the arame in warm water for 10 minutes, then drain and rinse. Soak the golden raisins and goji berries in the lemon juice for 10 minutes. Drain, reserving the lemon juice.

Beat together the flaxseed oil, cider vinegar, and reserved lemon juice. Combine all the salad ingredients together in a large mixing bowl, reserving a few toasted almond slivers for decoration.

## 290 Red cabbage, beet, and radish salad

V

Serves 4

### Ingredients
- 1 pound red cabbage
- 1 tablespoon soy sauce
- 2 tablespoons cider vinegar
- 2 beets
- 8 radishes
- 1 orange
- 1 blood orange
- 2 tablespoons olive oil
- Salt and freshly ground black pepper

### Preparation
Finely shred the cabbage and put it in a large mixing bowl with the soy sauce and cider vinegar. Use your hands to scrunch the cabbage and make sure it is well coated with the dressing. Peel and shred the beets, and shred the radishes. Zest one of the oranges, and reserve the zest. Then peel both oranges with a sharp knife to remove all white pith, and carefully cut into segments, avoiding the membranes that separate the segments. Gently combine all the ingredients and chill for a few minutes before serving.

*Many winter vegetables do not have to be cooked. Using them raw is the best way to preserve their nutrients, color, and texture. Potatoes are the exception and must always be cooked before eating.*

## 291 Roasted chestnut salad

Serves 4

### Ingredients
- 1 ½ cups wheat berries
- 1 cup roasted chestnuts
- 3 carrots
- 3 scallions
- Small handful fresh mint
- 1 tablespoon soy sauce
- 3 tablespoons white wine vinegar
- 1 tablespoon olive oil
- ½ cup raisins

### Preparation
Put the wheat berries in a bowl, cover with water and soak overnight. Drain and rinse the wheat berries, then put in a 3-quart pan, cover with water and bring to a boil. Reduce the heat and simmer for one hour, until the wheat berries become tender and begin to break open. Drain.

Roughly chop the chestnuts, shred the carrots, then finely chop the scallions and mint. Beat the soy sauce, wine vinegar, and olive oil together, then stir in the wheat berries. Add the chestnuts, shredded carrots, chopped scallions, raisins, and mint, and toss well to combine. Serve immediately.

*Wheat "berries" are simply grains of whole wheat. They're rich in fiber and have a chewy texture.*

# Five ways with parsnips

## 292
### Roasted
Roasting parsnips brings out their sweetness. Simply peel and slice or dice, toss in olive oil and cook at 400°F for up to 40 minutes until tender and beginning to caramelize. Add aromatic toasted fennel or caraway seeds or a drizzle of truffle oil to really bring out the flavor.

## 293
### Mashed
Try mashing parsnips, or a mixture of two or three different root vegetables, such as rutabaga and potato. Enrich the taste with buttery roasted garlic, hot chili oil, or fresh pesto.

## 294
### In a cake
Just like carrots and pumpkins, parsnips are surprisingly sweet and can be used to make muffins and cakes. Combinations featuring maple syrup, hazelnuts, ginger, or lime all work well.

## 295
### In a soup or sauce
The classic combination is parsnip and apple, but Indian spices like cumin and garam masala work well too. Add a few tablespoons of coconut milk and a little hot chili powder to make a simple korma-style curry sauce.

## 296
### Rösti
Peel and shred parsnips, mix with seasoned flour spiced with a little paprika, turmeric, or cumin, and pan-fry in small patties.

# 297 Chestnut sausage rolls

Makes 12

### Ingredients

- 1 onion
- 1 clove garlic
- 1 cup canned unsweetened chestnut purée or cooked mashed chestnuts
- 1 tablespoon tomato paste
- 1 tablespoon soy sauce
- 2 cups fresh bread crumbs
- 1 teaspoon dried thyme
- 1 package puff pastry sheets

### Preparation

Preheat the oven to 375°F.

Peel the onion and finely chop. Peel and crush the garlic. Mix all the ingredients for the filling together thoroughly in a large bowl. Working on a floured board, cut the pastry into long strips about 2-inches wide. Make a line of filling about as thick as your little finger down the center of each pastry strip. Dampen one long edge of the pastry with a little water, roll up, and seal. Cut each long roll into mini rolls around 1-inch long. Transfer to a baking sheet lined with parchment paper, leaving room for them to puff up, then bake for 15 minutes, until golden.

*If you can't find cooked chestnuts in a grocery store near you, they can be bought online—or you can make these delicious rolls using the recipe for Mushroom and Sage Sausages on page 198 in place of the chestnut mixture.*

## 298 Cranberry and pear chutney

Serves 4

### Ingredients

- 1 small onion
- 1 pear
- 1 tablespoon red wine vinegar
- 1 tablespoon brandy
- ½ pound fresh or frozen cranberries
- ½ cup brown sugar
- ½ teaspoon apple pie spice
- ½ teaspoon ground cinnamon
- ½ teaspoon ground ginger

### Preparation

Peel the onion and chop it finely. Core the pear and chop it finely. Put the onion, pear, vinegar, and brandy in a 3-quart heavy pan and cook gently for 10 minutes, until the onion and pear have softened. Stir in the cranberries, sugar, and spices and cook for a further 15 minutes or so, until the cranberries split and the liquid is reduced to a thick consistency. Let cool, then store in a jar in the fridge for up to two weeks.

*This chutney is perfect with a cheese board, as a thoughtful gift, or to serve with snacks such as the Chestnut Sausage Rolls (left).*

## 299 Crunchy seed balls

Serves 4

### Ingredients

- ¾ cup sesame seeds
- ⅓ cup pumpkin seeds
- ⅓ cup sunflower seeds
- 2 teaspoons toasted sesame oil
- 2 teaspoons soy sauce
- 1 rib celery
- 3 teaspoons cider vinegar
- 1 tablespoon preserved fruit relish or chutney

### Preparation

Put the sesame seeds into a dry, heavy pan and warm them gently. As soon as they begin to change color, put them onto a cool plate to stop from cooking.

Put half of the sesame seeds and all the remaining ingredients into a food processor and process until the mixture holds together. Form it into 20 walnut-size balls, and roll in the remaining toasted sesame seeds to coat. Refrigerate for up to three hours to firm up before serving.

# 300 Crisp red and green salad

Serves 4

### Ingredients
- 1 carrot
- 2 ounces celery root
- Few sprigs fresh thyme
- Juice ½ lemon
- 2 tablespoons olive oil
- ½ pound mixed crisp red and green salad
- 3 tablespoons raw edamame beans
- 2 tablespoons cress

### Preparation

Peel the carrot and celery root, and use a julienne peeler to cut long, thin strips (you can use a knife, but if you are making a lot of salads, buying a julienne peeler is a good investment). Strip the leaves off the woody stems of the thyme. Mix the lemon juice and olive oil together.

To assemble the salad, toss the salad leaves together with the carrot, celery root, edamame, and thyme. Dress with the olive oil and lemon juice, and garnish with the cress.

*Edamame are raw soy beans. They are available frozen, and it's handy to have a bag in the freezer, as they are an exceptional source of protein for vegetarians. Thaw a handful by putting them into a sieve and pouring over a kettle of boiling water. Refresh them under cold running water if you want to use them cold.*

## 301 Kohlrabi and sweet potato pancakes

Serves 4

**Ingredients**

- 1 small kohlrabi
- 1 sweet potato
- 1 sprig fresh thyme
- 3 tablespoons chickpea (gram) flour
- Salt and freshly ground black pepper
- 1 large egg
- Vegetable oil, for the pan

**Preparation**

Peel the kohlrabi and sweet potato, and shred coarsely. Strip the thyme leaves from the woody stems and chop them finely. Transfer the shredded vegetables to a large bowl and stir in the fresh thyme, chickpea flour, and seasoning. Beat the egg and stir it into the mixture. Heat the oil in a heavy skillet. Drop teaspoons of the mixture onto the hot surface, flatten into small cakes and cook for up to three minutes on each side, until crisp and golden. Serve immediately, with a fruity chutney or relish.

*Kohlrabi is an under-used vegetable with a pleasant nutty flavor that marries beautifully with sweet potatoes. Both have a soft texture that contrasts with the crispy outer layer of these patties.*

## 302 Brown rice salad with dates and pomegranate

**V**

Serves 4

**Ingredients**

- ¾ cup brown rice
- 4 dried, pitted dates
- 4 scallions
- 1 teaspoon fennel seeds
- 1 teaspoon cumin seeds
- 2 tablespoons cashew nuts
- 2 tablespoons fresh pomegranate seeds
- 1 lemon
- 3 tablespoons olive oil

**Preparation**

Put the rice in a 3-quart pan of water, bring to a boil, reduce to a low heat, and simmer for 40 minutes, until tender. Drain and rinse with cold water.

Chop the dates and slice the scallions into fine rings. Crush the fennel and cumin seeds with a pestle and mortar or a rolling pin. Toast the cashews in a dry, heavy pan until they begin to color. Zest and juice the lemon.

Combine all the ingredients, cover and chill for at least 30 minutes to allow the flavors to develop.

# 303 Spiced winter pickles

Serves 4

**V**

## Ingredients

- 1 large cauliflower
- 3 onions
- 3 carrots
- 1 cucumber
- 1 red bell pepper
- 7 ounces green beans
- ½ cup salt
- ⅓ cup all-purpose flour
- 2 teaspoons curry powder
- 2 teaspoons ground turmeric
- 2 teaspoons mustard powder
- 2 teaspoons ground ginger
- 1 quart white wine vinegar
- ⅔ cup sugar

## Preparation

Trim the cauliflower and break it into small florets. Peel and dice the onions. Peel and slice the carrots. Peel, de-seed and slice the cucumber. De-seed the red bell pepper and slice into fine strips. Trim the beans and chop into 1-inch pieces. Put all the prepared vegetables into a large mixing bowl and toss with the salt. Transfer to a colander, cover, and leave in the kitchen sink for 12 hours or overnight. Then wash the vegetables well in several changes of water and put them back into the colander to drain thoroughly.

Put the flour and spices into a 6-quart or preserving pan and heat them gently, stirring constantly. Gradually pour in the vinegar, stirring all the time to make sure no lumps are formed. Stir in the sugar and bring to a boil—the mixture should thicken. Put the prepared vegetables into the pan, stir well to combine with the spicy sauce and cook for a further three minutes, until all the vegetables are hot.

Pour into sterilized jars and seal immediately. Leave for four weeks before using.

# 304 Warm red cabbage salad
Serves 4

## Ingredients
- 1 small red cabbage
- 2 shallots
- 1 green apple
- 2 scallions
- 2 to 3 sprigs fresh thyme
- 2 tablespoons olive oil
- ⅓ cup walnuts
- 3 ounces soft rindless goat cheese

## Preparation
Core and shred the cabbage. Peel and finely slice the shallots.
Core and thinly slice the apple. Chop the scallions, leaving
the green parts in pieces about 1 inch long. Strip the leaves
off the woody stems of the thyme.

Heat the oil in a 4-quart pan or wok and stir-fry the cabbage,
shallots, and walnuts for up to six minutes until the shallots
are soft and the cabbage is cooked but still crisp. Add the
apple slices to the cabbage mixture, stir-frying for a further
minute or two, until they are warmed through. Transfer
to a serving dish and dress with the thyme leaves and the
scallions. Tuck in small pieces of crumbled goat cheese and
serve while the cabbage is still warm.

*If not using the prepared apple immediately, you can put it in a
bowl of water with the juice of half a lemon, to prevent browning.
Remember to drain the slices well before using.*

## 305 Baked parsnips with sour cream

Serves 4

### Ingredients

- 1 pound parsnips
- 1 onion
- 2 cloves garlic
- 2 tablespoons vegetable oil
- 1¼ cups vegetable bouillon
- ½ teaspoon mustard
- ½ teaspoon paprika
- ⅔ cup sour cream
- 1 cup fresh bread crumbs
- 1 ounce Cheddar cheese

### Preparation

Preheat the oven to 400°F.

Peel the parsnips and slice them about ¼ inch thick. Peel and finely chop the onion. Peel and crush the garlic. Warm the oil in a 3-quart pan and gently sauté the onion for about five minutes, until it is soft and beginning to brown. Add the parsnips and sauté for a further five minutes, until they begin to color and soften. Stir in the garlic and cook for a minute or two before adding the bouillon, mustard, and paprika. Bring to a boil, then turn down the heat and simmer, covered, for 15 minutes.

Remove the pan from the heat and let cool slightly before stirring in the sour cream. Transfer to a baking dish, top with the bread crumbs and cheese, and then bake until crisp and golden, around 20 minutes.

## 306 Red cabbage with toasted pecans

Serves 4

### Ingredients

- ⅓ cup pecans
- 1 small red cabbage
- 1 red onion
- 1 shallot
- 2 tablespoons orange juice
- 1 tablespoon red wine vinegar
- 2 tablespoons olive oil

### Preparation

Toast the pecans in a dry, heavy pan for up to three minutes, until they begin to brown. As soon as they start to change color, remove the pan from the heat and turn the nuts onto a plate to stop them from cooking any further. Finely shred the cabbage, discarding the woody center. Peel and slice the onion. Peel and finely slice the shallot. Beat the orange juice, shallot, and vinegar together.

Heat the oil in a 4-quart pan or wok, and stir-fry the cabbage and red onions for three minutes, until hot but still quite firm. Stir in the pecans and dressing, toss to combine and heat through for a further minute before serving.

# 307 Stir-fried vegetable parcels with lemon cream

Serves 4

### Ingredients

- 1 package phyllo pastry
- ¼ cup salted butter
- 10 ounces mixed vegetables: baby corn, broccoli florets, fine green beans, bell peppers, asparagus and carrots
- 1 tablespoon vegetable oil

### For the sauce

- 1 clove garlic
- 1 tablespoon salted butter
- ½ cup light vegetable bouillon
- ½ cup half and half
- 1 tablespoon cornstarch
- 3 tablespoons lemon juice
- Freshly ground black pepper

### Preparation

Preheat the oven to 350°F. Cut 12 large circles from the pastry sheets using a dinner plate as a guide. Melt the butter and brush four of the pastry circles. Cover each with another piece of pastry and repeat to make four stacks of three pastry sheets. Put the pastry on a baking sheet lined with parchment paper and put a little crumpled parchment at the center of each circle. Carefully fold the edges of the pastry up around the parchment to create open pastry shells. Bake for up to eight minutes, until crisp and golden. Allow the pastry shells to cool before carefully removing the parchment.

Make the sauce. Peel and crush the garlic and sauté it gently in the butter for a minute. Stir in the bouillon and half and half. Bring the mixture to boiling point, then reduce the heat and simmer for three minutes. Mix the cornstarch with the lemon juice and beat this into the cream, stirring to prevent any lumps. Cook for a further two minutes, until the mixture is thickening, and season with black pepper.

Peel and chop the vegetables into bite-size pieces and stir-fry in the oil for five minutes until cooked through but still crisp. Arrange the hot cooked vegetables in and on top of the pastry shells. Reheat the lemon cream sauce and top each serving with a little sauce.

## 308 Cauliflower with tahini dressing

Serves 4

V

### Ingredients
- 1 cauliflower
- 2 teaspoons cumin seeds

### For the dressing
- Small handful fresh parsley
- Few sprigs fresh mint
- 2 teaspoons white wine vinegar
- 1 tablespoon light tahini
- Juice 1 lemon
- Salt and freshly ground black pepper

### Preparation
Trim the cauliflower, separate it into small florets and boil in lightly salted water for 10 minutes. Toast the cumin seeds in a dry, heavy pan until they release their aroma. Remove from the hot pan and set aside.

To make the dressing, finely chop the fresh herbs. Beat together the wine vinegar, tahini, lemon juice, herbs, and seasoning.

Drain the cauliflower and put in a warmed serving dish. Pour over the dressing, sprinkle with the toasted cumin seeds and serve immediately.

## 309 Cauliflower, leek, and navy bean casserole

Serves 4

### Ingredients
- 2 leeks
- 1 orange bell pepper
- ½ small cauliflower
- 2 tablespoons vegetable oil
- ½ teaspoon smoked paprika
- ½ x 15-ounce can navy beans
- ½ cup crème fraîche or sour cream
- ⅔ cup plain yogurt
- 1 ounce smoked Cheddar or other hard smoked cheese

### Preparation
Preheat the oven to 400°F.

Trim and finely slice the leeks De-seed and slice the bell pepper, divide the cauliflower into florets. In a 4-quart pan or wok, stir-fry the vegetables together with the vegetable oil and smoked paprika for five minutes.

Drain and rinse the beans, and mix together with the vegetables, crème fraîche, and yogurt. Transfer to a shallow baking dish. Shred the cheese over the top and bake for 15–20 minutes until golden and bubbling.

# 310 Creamy sunchokes with mushrooms

Serves 4

## Ingredients

- ½ pound sunchokes
- ½ pound button mushrooms
- 2 tablespoons vegetable oil
- 3 cloves garlic
- 1 teaspoon dried rosemary
- 1 teaspoon dried thyme
- ½ cup dry white wine
- 4 tablespoons heavy cream

## Preparation

Preheat the oven to 350°F.

Scrub the sunchokes and slice them finely. Wipe and slice the mushrooms.

Sauté the sunchokes and mushrooms gently in the oil for five minutes, until the mushrooms have released their juices and the mixture is no longer wet. Peel and crush the garlic, add it to the sunchokes and mushrooms and continue to cook for a further minute.

Stir in the herbs and wine, and simmer, covered, for five minutes, until the sunchokes are tender. Stir in the cream and heat through before serving.

*Sunchokes are an often overlooked member of the winter root family, and are a great alternative to potatoes or parsnips, with a nutty and sweet flavor. This rich and velvety dish would go perfectly with some green beans or cabbage as a hearty main, or could be served alongside a nut loaf as part of a winter dinner party spread.*

# 311 Corn fritters

Serves 4

## Ingredients
- 1¼ cups canned corn
- 4 scallions
- 1 large egg
- 2 tablespoons all-purpose flour
- Salt and freshly ground black pepper
- Vegetable oil, for the pan

## Preparation

Drain the corn and put it into a large mixing bowl. Trim and chop the scallions and add them to the corn. Separate the egg into white and yolk. Mix the yolk, flour, and seasoning into the corn. Beat the egg white into soft peaks and gently fold it into the corn mixture.

Heat a little oil in a skillet and pan-fry a tablespoon of the mixture, turning once, until crisp and golden on both sides. Repeat with the remaining batter, frying in batches. Serve immediately.

*Add some finely chopped fresh chili peppers to these fritters to warm you up on a cold day. When being cooked, the corn can spit and pop, so it's best to wear an apron and be prepared for some splashes.*

## 312 Turkish fried potatoes

Serves 4

### Ingredients
- 1 pound potatoes
- 2 onions
- 2 scallions
- Handful fresh parsley
- ½ tablespoon olive oil
- 1 tablespoon tomato paste
- ½ teaspoon hot paprika
- Juice ½ lemon
- Salt and freshly ground black pepper

### Preparation

Peel the potatoes, cut them into chunks if they are large, and boil them in salted water until cooked through but not disintegrating. When cool enough to handle, cut them into bite-size pieces. Peel and roughly chop the onion, and trim and chop the scallions. Chop the fresh parsley.

Warm the oil in a 3-quart pan and gently fry the onions and scallions until soft and translucent. Stir in the tomato paste and paprika, and mix the potatoes in thoroughly. Season, and cook until all the sauce has been absorbed by the potatoes. Dress the dish with lemon juice and parsley and serve hot or cold.

## 313 Honey-glazed root vegetable ribbons

Serves 4

### Ingredients
- 2 parsnips
- 4 carrots
- 1 orange
- 3 tablespoons honey
- 1 tablespoon sesame oil
- 1 tablespoon olive oil
- 2 tablespoons sesame seeds

### Preparation

Preheat the oven to 375°F.

Peel the parsnips and carrots and slice them, lengthwise, as thinly as you can. Parboil them in a 3-quart pan of boiling salted water for five minutes. Slice one half of the orange into thin rounds, and set aside. Zest and juice the other half of the orange. Warm the honey in a small pan. Drain the parsnips and carrots, and transfer to a large bowl. Toss with the honey, sesame oil, olive oil, sesame seeds, orange juice, and orange zest. Put the mixture in a shallow baking dish and cook in the oven for up to 20 minutes, until just brown. Serve decorated with the reserved orange slices.

## 314 Baked kale in creamy onion sauce

Serves 4

### Ingredients

- 3¼ pounds kale
- 5 onions
- 1 potato
- 2 cloves garlic
- 1 bay leaf
- 4 cloves
- 1 teaspoon nutritional yeast
- 3 vegetable bouillon cubes
- 3¾ cups 2% milk or soy milk
- Salt and freshly ground black pepper
- 2 tablespoons sunflower seeds

### Preparation

Preheat the oven to 375°F.

Chop the kale and discard any tough stems. Cook in a 3-quart pan of boiling water for 10 minutes. Peel and chop the onions. Peel the potato and cut into small dice. Bruise the garlic (crush it with the flat side of a knife) but keep the cloves whole. Put the chopped onion and potato, garlic, bay leaf, cloves, nutritional yeast, bouillon cubes, and milk in a 3-quart pan and simmer, covered, for 30 minutes, until the potatoes and onions are very soft. Remove the cloves, garlic, and bay leaf, and blend until smooth. Taste and season with salt and pepper.

Drain the kale and arrange it in a baking dish. Pour the sauce over, sprinkle with the sunflower seeds, and then bake for 20 minutes until golden and bubbling.

## 315 Spicy tomato sauce

Serves 4

### Ingredients

- 1 onion
- 4 cloves garlic
- 1 tablespoon olive oil
- 2 x 15-ounce can diced tomatoes
- 1 teaspoon cinnamon
- 1 tablespoon apple cider, juice or hard cider
- 1 tablespoon lemon juice
- Salt and freshly ground black pepper

### Preparation

Peel and finely chop the onion. Peel and crush the garlic. Heat the oil in a saucepan and gently sauté the onion until soft and translucent. Stir in the garlic and cook for another minute, then add the diced tomatoes, cinnamon, cider, and lemon juice. Simmer for 10 minutes and season to taste with salt and pepper. This sauce would be the perfect companion served hot with the Stuffed Cabbage on page 266.

## 316 Kale and ginger stir-fry

Serves 4

### Ingredients
- 2 pounds kale, preferably cavolo nero
- 1 inch ginger root
- 1 tablespoon fennel seeds
- 6 tablespoons olive oil
- ½ teaspoon dried red pepper flakes
- Salt and freshly ground black pepper

### Preparation
Wash the kale and trim away the thickest stems. Shred the leaves. Shred the ginger.

Roast the fennel seeds for one minute in a dry skillet or wok. Then add the oil, shredded ginger, red pepper flakes, and seasoning to the pan and cook for up to three minutes. Add the shredded kale and stir-fry for five minutes. Season to taste with salt and freshly ground black pepper.

*Cavolo nero is a dark-leaved variety of kale, traditionally an important source of fresh vitamins in the depths of winter as it survived very cold weather!*

## 317 Kale with caramelized shallots

Serves 4

### Ingredients
- 2 pounds kale
- 10 shallots
- ¼ cup olive oil
- Salt and freshly ground black pepper

### Preparation
Wash and shred the kale. Cook in a 3-quart pan of boiling water for five minutes, then drain. Peel and finely slice the shallots. In a 3-quart pan, sauté the shallots in the olive oil until meltingly soft and golden brown. Stir in the cooked kale, and toss together to spread the flavored oil and shallots through the dish. Stir-fry for up to three minutes, until warmed through. Season to taste with salt and freshly ground black pepper.

## 318 Broccoli and orange stir-fry

Serves 4

### Ingredients
- 2 tablespoons sunflower seeds
- 1 tablespoon soy sauce
- 4 oranges
- 1¾ pounds broccoli
- 3 tablespoons canola oil
- 1 teaspoon fennel seeds
- Salt and freshly ground black pepper

### Preparation

Toast the sunflower seeds in a heavy pan for three minutes. Splash the soy sauce into the pan and stir quickly to coat the seeds before the liquid sizzles away. Remove from the heat. Shred the zest from two of the oranges and squeeze out the juice. Cut the peel off the other two oranges and cut them into segments. Cut the broccoli into bite-size florets. Chop up the stems too, discarding any particularly thick and woody pieces.

Heat the oil in a 4-quart pan or wok, and stir-fry the broccoli with the orange zest and fennel seeds for five minutes. Reduce the heat and pour in the orange juice. Cook gently for a further eight minutes or so, until the broccoli is just tender. Season with salt and pepper, and toss the orange segments and sunflower seeds through the broccoli before serving.

## 319 Pasta arrabbiata with broccoli

Serves 4

### Ingredients
- 1 pound broccoli
- ½ pound whole-wheat pasta
- 1 red bell pepper
- 1 red chili pepper
- 2 cloves garlic
- ¼ cup olive oil
- 1 teaspoon freshly ground black pepper
- Chili oil, optional

### Preparation

Trim the broccoli into florets and cook in boiling water until just tender. Cook the pasta in salted boiling water until just tender, and drain.

De-seed and chop the pepper and chili pepper. Peel and chop the garlic. Heat the olive oil in a 3-quart pan. Add the chili pepper, red bell pepper, garlic, and black pepper, and cook for one minute. Add the drained, cooked broccoli florets and pasta, toss together thoroughly and continue to cook until the dish is piping hot. Dress with a little chili oil to serve.

# Five ways with cabbage

## 320
### Raw

Shred the leaves and let them wilt in a marinade of cider vinegar, some flavorful oil (such as walnut), a little sweetener (honey or maple syrup) and a dash of mustard or soy sauce.

## 321
### Stir fried

Sizzle some finely chopped garlic or ginger, or aromatic seeds such as cumin, fennel, or caraway in a wok before adding shredded cabbage leaves. Sauté until soft and add a splash of citrus juice.

## 322
### Stuffed

Blanch the leaves first to make them more pliable, and make sure the filling is strongly flavored, as you will only get a little taste in each bite. Steam the parcels or bake in a sauce until tender.

## 323
### Deep-fried

The crispy seaweed served in Chinese restaurants is actually deep-fried shredded cabbage. Dry the leaves well before immersing them in hot oil for a few seconds in small batches. Drain on paper towels before seasoning with salt and sugar.

## 324
### Juiced

Cabbage juice is rich in nutrients, but bitter-tasting, so dilute it with the juice of apples, oranges, carrots, or pomegranates, or add some fresh mint as you feed it through the juicer.

## 325 Sweet potato, parsnip, and carrot tagine

Serves 4

### Ingredients

- ½ pound sweet potatoes
- ½ pound parsnips
- ½ pound baby carrots
- 6 shallots
- 1 inch ginger root
- 2 tablespoons olive oil
- 2 cups vegetable bouillon
- 1 tablespoon honey or maple syrup
- 1 cinnamon stick
- ¾ cup pitted prunes
- Salt and freshly ground black pepper

### Preparation

Preheat the oven to 350°F.

Peel the sweet potatoes and parsnips and chop them into large pieces. Peel the carrots, peel and halve the shallots, and peel and mince or finely chop the ginger.

Heat a flameproof casserole dish on the stove, and cook the shallots in the oil until softened. Stir in the sweet potatoes, carrots, and parsnips and cook, stirring occasionally, for 10 minutes. Pour in the bouillon and add the honey or maple syrup, ginger, cinnamon stick, prunes, and salt and pepper. Cover and transfer to the oven. Cook for 30 minutes, stir the mixture, and return to the oven, uncovered, for a further 15 minutes. Serve over warm rice or couscous.

## 326 Shredded greens with pomegranate

Serves 4

### Ingredients

- 4 pounds greens: kale, green cabbage or collard greens
- 1 tablespoon canola oil
- ⅓ cup pomegranate seeds

### For the dressing

- 1 orange
- ¼ ounce crystallized ginger
- 2 tablespoons maple syrup
- 2 tablespoons olive oil
- 1 tablespoon white wine vinegar

### Preparation

Make the dressing first. Juice the orange and finely chop the crystallized ginger. Beat the juice together with the maple syrup, olive oil, ginger, and vinegar.

Trim and shred the greens. Heat the canola oil in a 4-quart pan or wok and stir-fry the greens for four minutes, until bright green and wilting. Toss the dressing through and serve immediately, topping each serving with pomegranate seeds.

# 327 Squash and sweet potato lasagna

Serves 4

## Ingredients

- 2 pounds butternut squash
- 1 pound sweet potatoes
- 2 onions
- 1 tablespoon olive oil
- 1 quart 2% milk
- ¼ teaspoon nutmeg
- 1 bay leaf
- 3 tablespoons all-purpose flour
- 5 ounces vegetarian Parmesan-style cheese
- Salt and freshly ground black pepper
- 1 package no-boil lasagna noodles
- 5 ounces mozzarella cheese

## Preparation

Preheat the oven to 450°F. Peel and chop the squash and sweet potato into bite-size pieces. Peel and coarsely chop one of the onions. Put these into a bowl and toss with the olive oil to coat all of the pieces. Turn the vegetables onto a baking sheet and roast for 30 minutes, until tender. Turn the oven down to 375°F.

Peel and roughly chop the other onion. Put in a saucepan with the milk, nutmeg, and bay leaf. Heat to a simmer, remove from the heat and leave to infuse for 15 minutes. Strain and discard the solids. Return the milk to the pan and beat in the flour. Cook over a medium heat for around 10 minutes, until the mixture thickens, then stir in the Parmesan-style cheese and season.

Spread a quarter of the cheese sauce mixture into the base of a rectangular dish. Cover with a layer of noodles, then half of the roasted vegetables. Slice the mozzarella and use a third of it to cover the vegetables. Pour a third of the remaining sauce over the top. Layer again with pasta, the remaining vegetables, half the remaining mozzarella and half the remaining sauce. Cover with a final layer of pasta, then the last of the sauce and mozzarella.

Cover the dish with aluminum foil and bake for 20 minutes. Remove the foil, and bake for a further 20 minutes, until the top of the lasagna is golden and bubbling.

# 328 Brussels sprouts with sherry-soaked cranberries

Serves 4

## Ingredients

- 3 tablespoons dried cranberries
- ¾ cup sweet sherry
- 3 tablespoons pistachios in shells
- ½ shallot
- 1 tablespoon sherry vinegar
- 1 teaspoon wholegrain mustard
- 1 tablespoon olive oil
- 4 pounds Brussels sprouts
- 1 tablespoon canola oil
- Salt and freshly ground black pepper

## Preparation

Put the dried cranberries in a 1-quart saucepan with the sherry and bring to a boil. Turn to the lowest heat available and cook for 10 minutes. Set aside to cool to room temperature.

Shell the pistachios. Peel and finely chop the shallot, then make a dressing by beating together the sherry vinegar, mustard, olive oil, and shallot. Cut the bottoms off the Brussels sprouts and separate them into individual leaves. Heat the canola oil in a 4-quart pan or wok and stir-fry the Brussels sprout leaves on a high heat for up to three minutes, moving them around constantly, until some of the leaves start to show brown patches.

Toss the dressing through the hot leaves, season, and serve immediately, garnishing each serving with cranberries, their remaining soaking liquid, and whole pistachios.

## 329 Saffron-spiced cauliflower
Serves 4

**Ingredients**
- ½ cup golden raisins
- Juice 1 orange
- ¼ cup olive oil
- Pinch saffron strands
- 1 cauliflower
- 1 onion
- 3 cloves garlic
- 1 teaspoon white wine vinegar
- 1 teaspoon paprika
- Salt and freshly ground black pepper
- Few springs fresh cilantro

**Preparation**
Put the golden raisins and orange juice in a small bowl and leave to soak. Put half of the olive oil into a small bowl with the saffron and leave to infuse. Trim the cauliflower and divide into florets. Blanch in a pan of boiling water for up to three minutes, until just tender. Drain and set aside.

Peel and finely chop the onion and garlic. In a 3-quart pan, sauté the onion in the remaining oil until soft, then add the garlic and cauliflower. Cook for a further three minutes, then reduce the heat, sprinkle the paprika into the mixture and pour in the saffron and the oil. Stir thoroughly to coat the vegetables, then add the vinegar and cook for another three minutes. Finally, add the golden raisins and orange juice. Stir to combine and continue to cook until the liquid is reduced. Season to taste with salt and pepper, and garnish with fresh cilantro before serving.

## 330 Trofie pasta with pesto

Serves 4

### Ingredients
- 12 ounces trofie pasta
- ½ pound baby potatoes
- 4 ounces green beans, trimmed
- ¼ cup sage pesto (see page 270)
- Vegetarian shredded cheese, to serve

### Preparation
Peel the potatoes and boil, with the pasta, in a 3-quart pan of salted water for five minutes. Trim the beans and cut them into short pieces. Add these to the pan and continue to boil for a further five minutes, until the potatoes are cooked and the pasta is al dente. Drain the pasta, potatoes, and beans, and return to the pan. Stir in the sage pesto. Serve with a bowl of shredded cheese so that everybody can help themselves.

*This is a classic combination that is loved in the Genoa region of Italy. Trofie pasta is said to resemble pigs' tails. Sometimes it is made with chestnut flour, so use this if you can find it, although other pasta would work in this dish too.*

## 331 Leek and apple pilaf

Serves 4

### Ingredients
- 1 leek
- ¾ cup brown rice
- 1¼ cups vegetable bouillon
- 1 cup apple cider, juice or hard cider
- 1 apple
- ½ cup hazelnuts

### Preparation
Trim the leek and slice it thinly. Mix together the rice, chopped leek, vegetable bouillon, and cider in a 2-quart pan. Bring to a boil, reduce the heat to the lowest possible setting, cover the pan and cook without stirring for 40 minutes.

Peel, core, and finely chop the apple. Sprinkle the apple pieces on top of the rice, replace the lid of the pan and continue to cook for up to 10 minutes more, until the rice is tender and the liquid has been absorbed. Remove from the heat and leave to stand, covered, for five minutes before fluffing with a fork. Chop the hazelnuts and sprinkle them over the top of the dish before serving.

# 332 Stroganoff potatoes
Serves 4

## Ingredients
- 4 baking potatoes
- 2 ounces button mushrooms
- 2 onions
- 6 inch piece kombu seaweed, optional
- 2 tablespoons olive oil
- 4 ounces firm tofu
- 2 tablespoons red wine vinegar
- 2 tablespoons tahini
- 2 tablespoons soy sauce
- 2 tablespoons arrowroot

## Preparation
Preheat the oven to 400°F. Scrub the potatoes and prick the skins with a fork. Bake for approximately one hour, depending on their size, until the skins are crisp and the flesh is soft all the way through.

Wipe and trim the button mushrooms. Peel and chop the onion. Put the kombu (if using) into a saucepan with 2½ cups of water, bring to a boil, cover, and simmer for 10 minutes. Remove the kombu and set aside to dry.

Warm the oil in a 3-quart pan and gently sauté the onions and mushrooms until the mushrooms begin to release their juices. Add half the kombu bouillon (save the rest to add to another soup or stew). Drain and press the tofu, and cut it into bite-size pieces. Gently stir the tofu into the pan, cover, and simmer on a very low heat for 20 minutes.

Mix the vinegar, tahini, soy sauce, and arrowroot together, stir into the stroganoff mixture and simmer for a further three minutes, or until the sauce thickens.

Cut the baked potatoes in half and divide the stroganoff mixture between them.

*Kombu is a sea vegetable that adds a rich savory taste to vegetarian dishes. It can be used more than once to make bouillon in this way—allow it to dry out between uses.*

## 333 Spinach roulade

Serves 4

### Ingredients

- 1¼ cups cooked spinach
- 4 ounces onion
- 4 large eggs
- 4 ounces vegetarian Parmesan-style cheese
- ¼ stick salted butter
- ¼ cup all-purpose flour
- ⅔ cup 2% milk
- 6 ounces cream cheese
- Salt and freshly ground black pepper
- Pinch nutmeg

### Preparation

Preheat the oven to 375°F. Grease and line a 13 x 19-inch jelly roll pan with parchment paper.

To make the filling, first finely chop the spinach and onion. Separate the eggs. Shred the Parmesan-style cheese finely. In a large, heavy pan, melt the butter. Stir in the flour and cook for a minute, then gradually stir in the milk. As the sauce thickens, remove a tablespoon of the mixture and reserve. Mix in the onion, cook for three minutes, then stir in the cream cheese until all the ingredients are combined. Season with nutmeg, salt, and pepper, and set aside.

To make the roulade, put the spinach into a food processor with the egg yolks and reserved sauce, season with salt and pepper and blend briefly until well mixed. Transfer to a large mixing bowl. In a separate bowl, beat the egg whites until they form stiff peaks and then gently fold them into the spinach mixture. Spoon the mixture into the pan and smooth it out. Bake for 15 minutes until risen and springy to touch.

Cover your work surface with a large sheet of parchment paper, sprinkled with the Parmesan-style cheese. While the roulade is still hot, turn it out of the pan and onto the parchment and slowly roll up. When you are ready to serve, carefully unroll the roulade, and spread the filling over it. Re-roll, and transfer to a serving plate. Serve warm or cold with the Spicy Tomato Sauce (see page 249).

# 334 Chestnut and sweet potato loaf

Serves 4

### Ingredients

- 2 onions
- 2 cloves garlic
- 1 tablespoon olive oil
- 3 sweet potatoes
- ½ stick salted butter
- 1 pound fresh spinach
- 1 teaspoon ground nutmeg
- Sprig fresh rosemary
- ½ pound roasted chestnuts
- ⅓ cup walnuts
- 1 large egg
- 2 cups fresh bread crumbs
- 1 tablespoon sun-dried tomato paste

### Preparation

Preheat the oven to 350°F. Grease a 9 x 5-inch loaf pan.

Peel and dice the onions, and peel and chop the garlic. Sauté the onions in the olive oil until soft, add the garlic and continue to cook for a further minute or two. Remove from the heat. Peel the sweet potatoes and chop into small chunks. Cook in boiling water until tender, drain and mash with half of the butter. Cook the spinach in a 3-quart pan with a little water until wilted. Drain, cool slightly, then finely chop. Mix in the remaining butter and ground nutmeg. Strip the rosemary leaves from the woody stems and finely chop. Peel the chestnuts, and roughly chop the chestnuts and walnuts. Beat the egg. Mix together the bread crumbs, chestnuts, walnuts, sun-dried tomato paste, chopped rosemary, and egg. Add the cooked onions and garlic, and the mashed sweet potato, and mix well.

Put half of the nut roast mixture into the prepared loaf pan, and cover it with the cooked, chopped spinach. Put the remaining nut roast mixture on top, smooth the surface and cover with aluminum foil. Bake for 30 minutes, then remove the foil and return to the oven for a further 10 minutes to brown. Let stand in the pan for 10 minutes before turning out.

*Look for vacuum-packed or frozen chestnuts if you can find them, as they are easy to use and keep well.*

## 335 Baked squash with spiced couscous

Serves 4

### Ingredients

- 2 small acorn squash (or other small winter squash)
- 2 tablespoons olive oil
- 1 cup couscous
- Pinch saffron strands
- 3 tablespoons dried cherries
- 1/3 cup pistachios
- 1 teaspoon harissa paste
- 1 teaspoon ras-el-hanout, optional
- Small handful fresh cilantro
- Melted butter, to serve

### Preparation

Preheat the oven to 400°F.

Cut the tops off the squashes, scoop out the seeds and brush the insides with olive oil. Put on a baking sheet and roast for up to 40 minutes (depending on size of squash) until tender. Put the couscous in a shallow bowl with the saffron strands and pour over a cup boiling water. Leave for 15 minutes until the water is absorbed, then fluff the couscous gently with a fork and transfer to a large mixing bowl. Mix in the dried cherries, pistachios, harissa paste, and ras-el-hanout (if using). Finely chop the cilantro and stir into the stuffing mix. Fill the squashes with the stuffing and return to the oven for a further 10 minutes. Spoon a little melted butter on top before serving.

*Ras-el-hanout is an aromatic Moroccan spice blend that includes dried rose petals. Meaning "head of the shop" in Arabic, the blend traditionally includes the best spices that a shopkeeper has on sale.*

# Five ways with beets

## 336
### Make a statement
Make a shocking-pink risotto, a ruby-red borscht, or team beets with soft, white goat cheese in a green salad. Golden and striped varieties are available and these look great very thinly sliced and drizzled with balsamic syrup and fresh green herbs.

## 337
### Roast it
When roasting, leave the skin on until it is cooked—it will then rub off easily, and it stops the color of the beet from bleeding into any other vegetables. Depending on their size, beets need a long time in the oven—60 to 90 minutes at 400°F.

## 338
### Crunchy chips
Deep-fry very thinly sliced beets, parsnips, and sweet potatoes in small batches. Cook the beets last, so all your chips don't turn pink! Drain on paper towels and sprinkle with salt and pepper.

## 339
### Shred it
Using a zester, julienne peeler, or potato peeler, you can create strips of raw beets and carrots that look beautiful in a green salad.

## 340
### Juice
Beet juice is super healthy and adds great color to a drink. Try combining it with apple or grape juice for sweetness, or with orange or grapefruit, to contrast the earthiness of the beet.

## 341 Winter vegetable hotpot
Makes 4

### Ingredients
- 1 pound rutabaga
- 1 small turnip
- 2 carrots
- 1 large onion
- 4 ounces button mushrooms
- ½ pound tomatoes
- 1 tablespoon miso paste
- 2½ cups vegetable bouillon
- ½ teaspoon cayenne pepper
- ½ teaspoon ground cinnamon

### Preparation
Preheat the oven to 350°F.

Peel the rutabaga, turnip, carrots, and onion, and slice them all thinly. Wipe the mushrooms. Peel and chop the tomatoes (see below).

Put all the vegetables into a casserole dish. Mix the miso paste with a little warm bouillon, then pour it into the pan and stir in the spices. Cover and bake for 90 minutes.

*To peel tomatoes, prick the skins with a sharp knife and put them into a heatproof bowl. Cover them with boiling water and leave for a few minutes—the skins should start to split. Pour off the hot water and cover the tomatoes with cold water. The skins should loosen up and slide off easily. Don't leave the tomatoes in the boiling water too long as they will start to cook!*

## 342 Fennel with ginger and orange sauce
Makes 4

### Ingredients
- 1 large head fennel
- 1 clove garlic
- 1 inch ginger root
- 4 scallions
- 2 tablespoons vegetable oil
- 1 orange
- 1 teaspoon soy sauce

### Preparation
Cut the fennel into quarters and steam it for up to 10 minutes, until just tender. Peel and crush the garlic, shred the ginger, and trim and chop the scallions. Zest and juice the orange. Warm the oil in a skillet and gently cook the scallion for three minutes, until soft. Stir in the garlic and ginger. Cook for a further minute, then add the orange juice and zest and the soy sauce. Heat through and pour over the warm fennel to serve.

# 343 Stuffed cabbage

Serves 4

### Ingredients
- ¾ cup mixed wild and basmati rice
- 1 onion
- 4 cloves garlic
- ½ cup apple cider, juice or hard cider
- ¾ cup raisins
- 1 small head Savoy cabbage
- 2½ cups vegetable bouillon

### Preparation
Preheat the oven to 350°F.

Put the rice into a 2-quart pan, cover with water and bring to a boil. Reduce the heat to a bare simmer, cover, and cook for 50 minutes, adding more water if necessary until the wild rice is tender. Drain and let cool. Peel and finely chop the onion. Peel and crush the garlic. Put the apple cider into a small pan and gently sauté the onion, garlic, and raisins in it until the onion is soft. Stir the mixture into the rice and mix thoroughly.

Prepare a 4-quart pan of boiling water. Trim the stalk of the cabbage and pull off all the leaves that are large enough to stuff—there are likely to be 12 to 15. Drop the leaves into boiling water and leave for five minutes to soften. Drain, and stuff each one with a spoonful of the rice mixture. Working on a flat surface, smooth out a leaf, put the stuffing in the center and fold up the sides, then roll up. You can trim away any thick stems that make rolling difficult. Pour a little bouillon into the bottom of a baking dish and arrange the cabbage rolls on top, making several layers if necessary. Pour the rest of the bouillon over the dish, cover with a lid or foil and bake for 30 minutes.

*Deceptively simple to prepare and always admired, stuffed cabbage can be filled with spiced rice and kept in the oven on a low heat until needed. They're best served with a colorful tomato or cranberry relish.*

# 344 Sweet potato gratin

Serves 4

### Ingredients

- 2 pounds sweet potatoes
- 1 onion
- 1 tablespoon olive oil
- Salt and freshly ground black pepper
- ½ cup salted butter
- 2 tablespoons all-purpose flour
- 1 ¼ cups 2% milk
- ⅔ cup half and half
- ½ teaspoon ground nutmeg
- ¼ cup pecans
- 1 cup fresh bread crumbs

### Preparation

Preheat the oven to 375°F.

Peel the sweet potatoes, cut them into large pieces and cook in boiling water for 25 minutes, until tender. Peel and finely chop the onion. Warm the oil and gently sauté the onion until it is soft and translucent.

Grease a baking dish. Slice the sweet potatoes thickly and arrange a layer in the bottom of the dish. Cover with half of the onions and season with salt and pepper. Add a second layer of sweet potatoes and a second layer of onions. Season once more.

Melt the butter in a 2-quart pan, stir in the flour and cook for a minute before beating in the milk and half and half. Bring to a boil, mix in the nutmeg and simmer for three minutes. Pour the sauce over the vegetables. Finely chop the pecans and sprinkle over the top of the dish with the bread crumbs. Bake for 30 minutes, until golden and bubbling.

# 345 Celery gratin with white wine and walnuts

Serves 4

### Ingredients

- 2 heads celery
- 1 onion
- 2 tablespoons olive oil
- 2 bay leaves
- ½ cup white wine
- 1 cup vegetable bouillon
- ½ cup heavy cream
- ⅓ cup walnuts
- ¼ stick salted butter
- 2 cups fresh bread crumbs
- 1 ounce vegetarian Parmesan-style cheese

*Celery is not just for salads and soups—here, it is the "hero" ingredient. Simmered with bay leaves, bubbled with wine, baked in cream, and topped with crispy bread crumbs … it's a celebration.*

### Preparation

Trim the celery and cut each stalk into 2-inch pieces. Peel the onion and slice thinly. Warm the olive oil in a heavy pan. Stir in the celery, onion, and bay leaves, reduce the heat to minimum, cover, and cook for 20 minutes, stirring occasionally. Stir in the wine and bouillon, turn the heat to high and cook for up to eight minutes to reduce the liquid by two-thirds. Stir in the cream and continue to cook on a high heat for five minutes until the sauce is quite thick.

Roughly chop the walnuts. Melt the butter in a pan, stir in the bread crumbs and walnuts, then stir over a medium heat for five minutes until golden brown. Shred the cheese. Preheat the broiler to high. Transfer the celery into a baking dish, remove the bay leaves and top with the bread crumbs and cheese. Put under the hot broiler for three minutes or so, until browned and crisp. Serve immediately.

# 346 Gnocchi with sage pesto

Serves 4

### Ingredients

- 2¼ pounds potatoes
- 1 large egg
- Salt and freshly ground black pepper
- 2½ cups all-purpose flour

### For the pesto

- ½ cup hazelnuts
- 2½ ounces fresh spinach
- 2 cloves garlic
- ⅓ cup olive oil
- 10 fresh sage leaves
- ½ teaspoon ground nutmeg
- Salt and freshly ground black pepper

### Preparation

Boil the potatoes in their skins until tender. Drain, let cool slightly, then peel away and discard the skins. Beat the egg. Mash the potatoes with the egg and seasoning. Transfer to a large mixing bowl and stir in 1½ cups of the flour. Turn the mixture onto a floured work surface or board. Gently knead the dough, gradually bringing in the remaining flour. This should only take a minute or two, don't overwork the dough. Divide the dough into four pieces and gently roll each one into a sausage shape. Cut into 1-inch pieces and refrigerate on a floured tray until needed.

To make the pesto, toast the hazelnuts in a dry pan for two minutes, and let cool completely. Put the nuts in a food processor with the fresh spinach, garlic, and half of the olive oil. Process to a rough paste, using the pulse function, gradually adding the remaining oil. Add the sage leaves and nutmeg, and pulse to combine. Season with salt and pepper.

Bring a 4-quart pan of salted water to a boil. Drop the gnocchi into the water, working in small batches so that the temperature of the water does not fall. The gnocchi is cooked when it rises to the surface. Scoop it out with a slotted spoon and serve immediately with the sage pesto.

# 347 Chestnut and red wine casserole

Serves 4

### Ingredients

- 2 parsnips
- 1 sweet potato
- 6 ounces shallots
- 1 medium eggplant
- 1 zucchini
- 2 red bell peppers
- 2 leeks
- 6 ounces button mushrooms
- 3 tablespoons olive oil
- ½ pound tomatoes
- 3 ounces cooked, peeled chestnuts
- 2 cloves garlic
- 2¾ cups puréed tomatoes or canned tomato sauce
- 2½ red wine
- 2 bay leaves
- ½ teaspoon cinnamon
- Salt and freshly ground black pepper

### Preparation

Peel the parsnips, sweet potato, and shallots, then chop them all into bite-size pieces. Chop the eggplant, zucchini, and red bell peppers, slice the leeks and trim and wipe the mushrooms. Heat the olive oil in a 4-quart, heavy pan and sauté the parsnips and sweet potato gently for 10 minutes, until soft. Stir in the shallots, peppers, eggplant, zucchini, leeks, and mushrooms. Cover and cook for a further five minutes.

Chop the tomatoes, halve the chestnuts and peel and crush the garlic. Stir these and all the remaining ingredients into the pan. Cook gently, covered, for a further 15 minutes. Adjust the seasoning with salt and pepper to taste.

# Five ways with chestnuts

## 348

**Simply roasted**

Preheat the oven to 400°F. Carefully cut a cross into the shiny outer skin of each chestnut. Spread them out in a roasting pan and roast for around 30 minutes, until they split open.

## 349

**Savory mixture**

Chopped, cooked chestnuts, or unsweetened chestnut purée can be used to make a nut loaf, or be combined with cranberries in a seasonal stuffing mix. Or, try wrapping a chestnut mixture in puff pastry to make a nut roast en croûte.

## 350

**Chestnut flour pancakes**

Make a gluten-free batter using 1 cup rice flour, ½ cup chestnut flour, 2 teaspoons baking powder, ½ teaspoon baking soda, 2 beaten eggs, ½ cup 2% milk, and a pinch of salt. Stack with layers of colorful spinach, beets, and squash for a seasonal treat.

## 351

**Soup**

Sauté carrot, parsnip, and celery root. Add cooked chestnuts, vegetable bouillon, a splash of sherry, and season with nutmeg. Purée, and top with chestnut pieces and a swirl of sour cream.

## 352

**Candied**

Marrons glacés are chestnuts candied in syrup. Eat them like candies, purée them, or chop them over vanilla ice cream.

## 353 Scandinavian mulled wine

Serves 6

### Ingredients
- ¼ cup vodka
- 1 cinnamon stick
- 5 whole cloves
- 1 bottle fruity red wine
- 1 teaspoon ground cinnamon
- ½ teaspoon ground ginger
- ½ cup brown sugar

### Preparation
Put the vodka into a 3-quart pan with the cinnamon stick and cloves, bring to simmering point and then set aside for at least an hour. When your guests arrive, pour in the wine and add the ground cinnamon, ginger and sugar. Serve warm.

*This Scandinavian-style mulled wine packs a punch! Traditionally, this is served with raisins, which are put into the bottom of the glasses before filling up. Leave some teaspoons next to the punch bowl so guests can spoon the fruit out and eat it once they've finished their drinks.*

## 354 Cranberry fizz

Serves 4

### Ingredients
- 2 cups sparkling apple juice
- 2 cups cranberry juice

### Preparation
Mix the two juices together and serve over ice.

*This is a welcoming cocktail at any holiday occasion. For an alcoholic version, add a splash of gin or vodka, or use sparkling hard apple cider or hard pear cider.*

## 355 Spiced chai tea

Serves 4

### Ingredients
- 1 inch ginger root
- 1 cinnamon stick
- 1 quart water
- ¾ teaspoon fennel seeds
- 3 cloves
- 6 cardamom pods
- 4 English breakfast teabags
- ½ cup 2% milk
- Honey or sugar to taste

### Preparation
Roughly chop the ginger and break the cinnamon stick into short pieces. In a small saucepan, bring the water to a boil, add the spices and ginger and simmer for 10 minutes. Put the teabags into the pan and simmer for another four minutes.

Warm the milk in a separate pan and pour it into the tea. Heat the mixture for a further two minutes, strain and serve. Add honey or sugar to taste.

## 356 Chili pepper hot chocolate

Serves 4

### Ingredients
- 1 red chili pepper
- 3 cups 2% milk
- 4 ounces semi-sweet chocolate
- ½ cup half and half

### Preparation
Slice the chili pepper in half lengthwise and de-seed. Put the milk into a pan and add the chili pepper. Bring the mixture to a simmer, then remove from the heat and allow to infuse for 10 minutes.

Break the chocolate into pieces. Reheat the milk, add the half and half and the chocolate, and continue to warm the mixture until the chocolate is completely melted. Remove the chili peppers just before serving.

# 357 Spicy chocolate chestnut cake

Serves 10

### Ingredients
- 4 large eggs
- ⅔ cup sugar
- 9 ounces semi-sweet chocolate
- 2¼ sticks unsalted butter
- 1 to 2 teaspoons chili powder, to taste
- 9 ounces cooked chestnuts
- 1 cup plus 2 tablespoons 2% milk
- 2 to 3 drops almond extract

### Preparation
Preheat the oven to 325°F. Grease and line a 9-inch springform cake pan with parchment paper.

Separate the eggs into yolks and whites and put them into separate mixing bowls. Beat the yolks with the sugar. Roughly chop the chocolate and put it into a small saucepan with the butter. Gently melt the chocolate and butter together. Stir in the chili powder and mix well to avoid any lumps. Let cool a little and then mix into the egg yolks and mix thoroughly.

Peel the chestnuts if they still have their outer skins on. Roughly chop and put them into a 1-quart pan with the milk. Bring to a boil, stir in the almond extract and let cool for a few minutes before transferring to a food processor. Process until smooth and add to the chocolate mixture, mixing well to prevent any pale streaks in the cake.

Beat the egg whites to soft peaks and gently fold them into the chocolate mixture. Spoon the mix into the prepared pan, smooth the top and bake for up to 45 minutes—it may still be a bit wobbly. Let cool before taking the cake out of the pan and slicing to serve.

*Chili peppers and chocolate have become a well-loved combination, especially appropriate for colder months. Thoroughly puréed chestnuts add a subtle sweet flavor and a grainy texture similar to ground almonds.*

## 358 Red velvet cupcakes
Makes 12

### Ingredients
- ½ pound cooked beets
- ⅓ cup canola oil
- 2 tablespoons lemon juice
- 1 teaspoon vanilla extract
- 4 tablespoons water
- 1½ cups all-purpose flour
- 1¾ cups sugar
- 3 tablespoons cocoa powder
- 1 teaspoon baking powder

### Preparation
Preheat the oven to 375°F. Grease a 12-cup muffin pan and line with paper liners.

Peel the beets, if necessary, and put it into a food processor with the oil, lemon juice, vanilla extract, and water. Blend to a smooth purée. Put the flour into a large bowl and mix together with the sugar, cocoa powder, and baking powder.

Stir the wet ingredients into the dry ingredients and mix to combine. Divide the mixture between the cups and bake for 20 minutes, until risen and cooked through. Let the cupcakes cool before decorating with your choice of extravagant frosting or melted vegan chocolate!

*Do not use beets preserved in vinegar for this recipe!*

## 359 Spiced raisin and banana muffins
Makes 12

### Ingredients
- 1 ripe banana
- 1 tablespoon apricot preserves
- 3 tablespoons raisins
- 1 large egg
- ½ cup 2% milk
- ½ cup canola oil
- 1 cup all-purpose flour
- 2 teaspoons baking powder
- ½ teaspoon apple pie spice
- 3 tablespoons brown sugar

### Preparation
Preheat the oven to 400°F. Grease a 12-cup muffin pan.

Mash the banana and mix with the apricot preserves and raisins in a small bowl. Whisk the egg, milk, and oil together and put the flour, baking powder, sugar, and apple pie spice into a large mixing bowl and stir together. Add the egg and milk mixture, then the banana and raisins. Stir until just blended—do not overmix, or your muffins will be too firm and springy.

Divide the mixture between the cups and bake for 30 minutes, until a skewer pushed into the center comes out clean. Cool on a wire rack.

# 360 Easy vegan fudge

Makes about 50 pieces

### Ingredients
- 3 ½ cups sugar
- 2 ½ cups soy milk
- 4 ounces vegan margarine
- 2 teaspoons vanilla extract

### Preparation

Line a 7-inch square pan with parchment paper. Half-fill your kitchen sink with cold water.

Put the sugar, soy milk, and margarine into a 3-quart heavy pan and heat gently to melt the margarine and dissolve the sugar. Bring to a boil and simmer until the temperature reaches 240°F on a sugar thermometer. If you don't have a sugar thermometer, prepare a small bowl of cold water. When the mixture is ready, a little of it dropped into the water will form a soft ball.

When this point is reached, quickly stir in the vanilla extract (or another flavoring of your choice), then carefully take the pan off the heat and put it into the cold water in the kitchen sink, to cool the mixture down quickly. Beat it with a wooden spoon until it becomes very thick, then pour it into the prepared pan, smooth the top and leave at room temperature to set. When it is firm, remove it from the pan and cut it into small pieces with a sharp knife.

*Overlap the parchment paper so that it hangs over the sides of the pan—this makes it easy to lift the fudge out when it has set.*

## 361 Fruity teabread

Serves 8

### Ingredients

- 1⅓ cups mixed dried fruit
- 1 cup freshly made black tea
- 2 cups self-rising flour
- 1 cup brown sugar
- 1 large egg
- 2 tablespoons orange marmalade

### Preparation

Put the dried fruit in a bowl, pour the tea on top and leave overnight to soak. Preheat the oven to 350°F. Grease and line a 10 x 6-inch loaf pan.

Sift the flour into a large bowl and stir in the sugar. Beat the egg and add it to the dry ingredients along with the marmalade, the soaked fruit and any remaining soaking liquid. Mix thoroughly. Spoon the mixture into the prepared pan, smooth the top and bake for one hour, until a skewer inserted into the cake comes out clean. Let cool in the pan for 10 minutes before turning onto a cooling rack. Let cool completely before slicing.

*Teabreads are traditional English cakes made with mixed dried fruit soaked overnight in black tea. Dense and moist, they are best baked in loaf pans and served sliced and buttered.*

## 362 Almond rice pudding

Serves 6

### Ingredients

- ½ cup pitted dates
- 1 cup brown rice
- 5 cups almond milk or soy milk
- 1 teaspoon almond extract
- ½ teaspoon ground cinnamon
- ⅔ cup raisins
- ½ cup toasted slivered almonds

### Preparation

Put the dates in a bowl and cover them with boiling water. Leave to soak for 15 minutes, then transfer the dates and water to a blender and blend until smooth. Put the rice and almond or soy milk into a 3-quart heavy pan, bring to a boil, then reduce the heat and simmer gently, stirring occasionally, for 45 minutes until the rice is cooked. Stir in the puréed dates, almond extract, cinnamon, raisins, and almonds.

## 363 Raspberry cranachan

Serves 4

### Ingredients

- 5 tablespoons oatmeal
- ⅔ cup heavy cream
- 2 tablespoons honey
- 2 tablespoons whiskey
- ⅔ cup crème fraîche or sour cream
- 14 ounces fresh raspberries

### Preparation

Preheat the broiler and line the broiler pan with aluminum foil. Spread the oatmeal evenly in the pan and broil for about three minutes, stirring occasionally, until golden. Let cool completely. Beat the cream until thick and fold in the crème fraîche. Stir in the honey and whiskey, and then mix in 4 tablespoons of the toasted oatmeal.

Put a few fresh raspberries in the base of four glass serving dishes, top with a little of the cream mixture and continue to layer the fruit and the cream, ending with a layer of cream in each dish and reserving a few raspberries for decoration. Sprinkle with the reserved toasted oatmeal and decorate with the remaining raspberries. Serve immediately.

*Cranachan is a traditional Scottish dessert. The splash of whiskey is essential—use Scotch if you can!*

## 364 Peanut butter truffles

Makes 18-20

### Ingredients

- ⅔ cup dates
- ⅔ cup walnuts
- 1 cup confectioners' sugar
- 1 cup vegan peanut butter (smooth or crunchy)
- 4 ounces vegan semi-sweet chocolate, plus extra shredded chocolate to decorate

### Preparation

Finely chop the dates and walnuts. Mix them together with the confectioners' sugar and peanut butter. Roll into truffle-sized balls and put on a parchment paper-lined baking sheet. Chill for up to 20 minutes. Roughly chop the chocolate and melt it in a small heatproof bowl over a saucepan of hot water.

Using a toothpick, dip the truffles into the melted chocolate, carefully put on the parchment paper and sprinkle with a little shredded chocolate. Return to the refrigerator until the chocolate has set firmly.

# 365 Sticky marmalade cake
Serves 8

## Ingredients
- 1 ½ sticks unsalted butter
- 1 ½ cups brown sugar
- 1 cup orange marmalade
- 2 large eggs
- ⅓ cup chopped crystallized ginger
- ⅓ cup chopped dates
- 1 teaspoon ground ginger
- 1 teaspoon ground pumpkin pie spice
- 1 ½ cups self-rising flour

## Preparation
Preheat the oven to 375°F. Grease and line a deep 9-inch cake pan.

Melt ½ stick of the butter in a small pan and stir in ½ cup of the sugar and ½ cup of the marmalade. Heat and stir until syrupy and then pour into the cake pan.

Beat the remaining butter and sugar together, then beat in the eggs. Chop the ginger and dates. Mix the spices into the flour and fold into the wet ingredients along with the candied ginger and dates. Fold in the remaining marmalade. Pour the cake mixture into the cake pan and spread it out over the marmalade syrup. Bake for one hour and 15 minutes, until just set. Allow to sit for 10 minutes before inverting onto a serving dish.

*If you plan to use a springform pan for this, take the precaution of lining the base with a piece of parchment paper that extends a little way up the sides of the pan, and put the pan onto a baking sheet before putting it into the oven, as it may leak.*

# Index

Page numbers marked in **bold** indicate "Five Ways With" entries.

# Acknowledgments

I'd like to thank Drew Smith for dreaming up the concept for the book, Clarissa Hyman for bringing Drew and I together, Silvia Langford for giving the project the green light and all the team at Elwin Street Productions for bringing it together. And my husband Gwilym Hughes for his patience.

# Picture credits

The publishers would like to thank the following for their permission to reproduce images.

Dreamstime: pp. 121 (Og-vision), 213 (Svetlana Kolpakova)

Getty Images: p. 104 (lois.slokoski.photography)

Alamy: p. 99 (Photocuisine)

iStock: pp. 4 (THEPALMER), 5 (Floortje), 9 third (fotogal), 13 (Cgissemann), 37 (FotografiaBasica), 61 (MmeEmil), 67 (bonchan), 71 (FuatKose), 76 (modedesigns58), 87 (Materio), 116 (AlasdairJames), 125 (Isantilli), 128 (JackJelly), 131 (Sarsmis), 151 sixth, 175 (YinYang), 168 (JensGade), 181 (RichLegg), 210 (hdagli), 215 (KevinDyer), 271 (Silberkorn)

Shutterstock: pp. 7 (Sergiy Akhundov), 9 first (nito) fifth (Aprilphoto) sixth (Ricardo Esplana Babor) seventh (Le Do) eighth (Igor Dutina), 9 second, 18 (First_emotion), 9 fourth, 151 first and fifth, 165, 177, 204 (KIM NGUYEN), 10 (Aprilpo), 15 (Valentina Proskurina), 22 (bonchan), 27 (Madlen), 30 (Oksana2010), 31, 113, 255 (Peter Zijlstra), 32, 72, 81 third and fifth, 206 (Nattika), 40 (Vorobyeva), 46, 81 second (Maks Narodenko), 44 (AN NGUYEN) 50, 171 (paulista), 51, 221 fourth, 239 (Egor Rodynchenko), 54 (Jessmine), 55 (Noraluca013), 64, 151 seventh (PhotoEd), 69 (Volosina), 81 first (StewfanoT) fourth (EM Arts) seventh (Anna Sedneva), 81 sixth, 108 (Hong Vo), 81 eighth, 122 (indigolotos), 82, 89, 221 fifth (Viktar Malyshchyts), 84 (nokkaew), 93 (ifong), 94 (Pack-Shot), 100 (Krasowit), 107 (Tom Wang), 109 (Scisetti Alfio), 119 (Igors Rusakovs), 127 (Andrey Starostin), 133 (Gerasimova Inga), 137 (matin), 141 (Guzel Studio), 145 (Martin Kubat), 146 (Luisa Puccini), 151 second (Yasonya) eighth(nito), 151 third, 170 (Tarasyuk Igor), 151 fourth, 185 (Only Fabrizio) 152 (joannawnuk), 156 (gresei), 161 (Dionisvera), 189 (Kenishirotie), 193 (cameilia), 199 (Natali Zakharova), 202 (Serhiy Shullye), 203 (Timmary), 204 (Africa Studio) 209 (schab), 218 (Jiri Hera), 221 second (julie deshaies) third (Evikka) eighth (HandmadePictures), 221 first, 222, 268 (Diana Taliun), 221 sixth, 234 (JIANG HONGYAN), 221 seventh, 250 (picturepartners), 223 (Helga Chirk), 227 (JackK), 231 (draconus), 233 (Chameleons Eye), 243 (amphaiwan), 245 (Oliver Hoffman), 252 (vipflash), 259 (haru), 263 (Green Art Photography), 264 (Arina P Habich), 269 (greatstockimages), 273 (sibadan), 274 (Tim UR), 279 (Yeko Photo Studio), 280 (Olga Popova)

Taste Library: pp 16, 21, 25, 29, 34, 39, 43, 48, 53, 56, 59, 62, 74, 79, 91, 103, 111, 115, 134, 139, 142, 149, 155, 159, 162, 167, 172, 179, 182, 186, 191, 195, 196, 201, 216, 225, 228, 236, 241, 246, 256, 261, 267, 276, 283